Property of
All Saints Episcopal Church
S. E. 41st · WOODSTOCK BLVD
PORTLAND, OREGON

THE CROSS STILL STANDS

The Friday of the Crucifixion

THE CROSS
STILL STANDS

The Friday of
the Crucifixion

by ALFRED DOERFFLER

BAKER BOOK HOUSE
Grand Rapids 6, Michigan
1960

THE CROSS STILL STANDS

———————————————

Copyright, 1960, by Baker Book House
Printed in the United States of America

First printing, November 1960

LIBRARY OF CONGRESS CATALOG CARD NUMBER: 60-16675

PHOTOLITHOPRINTED BY CUSHING - MALLOY, INC.
ANN ARBOR, MICHIGAN, UNITED STATES OF AMERICA
1960

FOREWORD

More and more Protestant ministers are preaching during the pre-Easter season on the Passion of our Lord, either at Sunday or midweek services. On the Friday of the Crucifixion events followed in rapid succession. These present excellent material for sermons with valuable lessons for our twentieth century Christians. These sermons may offer suggestions to such who seek to focus the spotlight on the cross which still stands in our world as the hope of all mankind in the hours of distress and despair.

Alfred Doerffler

CONTENTS

Where can I go to find a ray of hope
In shuffling through a world that's in despair?
Is there no star to guide me in the night,
No light to show my trembling soul the way?
    There is—the Star of Bethlehem.

I've travelled through a world that's in despair—
It gave me ashes when I asked for bread.
Is there no peace, no rest, no lasting joy,
No healing for my soul that's in distress?
    There is—in Christ of Calvary.

Is there a glory where my soul can dwell,
Away from this—a world that's in despair?
Where heartache, sorrow, death shall find no room,
And fear and want and hunger are unknown?
    There is—at Christ's eternal throne.

O Christ of Calvary, I've found that peace
Beneath Thy cross, where sin is blotted out.
Canst Thou not give this Gospel peace and hope
To all the world that's living in despair?
    "I can—through you."

1

THE ROAD TO THE CROSS

> *"And as they led Him away, they laid hold upon one*
> *Simon, a Cyrenian coming out of the country, and on*
> *him they laid the cross, that he might bear it after Jesus.*
> *And there followed Him a great company of people,*
> *and of women, which also bewailed and lamented Him.*
> *But Jesus turning unto them said, Daughters of*
> *Jerusalem, weep not for Me, but weep for yourselves,*
> *and for your children. For, behold, the days are coming,*
> *in which they shall say, Blessed are the barren, and the*
> *wombs that never bare, and the paps which never gave*
> *suck. Then shall they begin to say to the mountains,*
> *Fall on us; and to the hills, Cover us. For if they do these*
> *things in a green tree, what shall be done in the dry? And*
> *there were also two others, malefactors, led with Him to*
> *be put to death."*—Luke 23:26-32

The road to the cross is known as the Via Doloroso, the Way of Sorrows. It led to Calvary from the Gabbatha of Pontius Pilate in Jerusalem. The street was crowded with people from all walks of life, many of which had come from far-away parts of the Roman Empire. Most of these had come to Jerusalem to observe the annual Passover, commemorating Israel's escape from the bondage of Egypt in the days of Moses. The crowd was in a festive mood and curious, restless and looking for excitement. All of them were seemingly eager to join any form of diversion to break the monotony of the hour. Some had come from Galilee and the still further Damascus; others from Greece and Rome and Egypt. You saw in the motley crowd men from Babylon on the Euphrates and from the distant city of Cyrene in northern Africa.

Coming along this road was One Jesus, dragging a cross up the hill of Calvary. He had just been condemned to be crucified. The night had been hectic through which this Jesus has passed. Betrayed, arrested, He had been tried in two courts, that of the highpriest Caiaphas and that of the Governor Pontius Pilate. He had been beaten at the whipping post, crowned with thorns, and abused by ruthless soldiers who were seeking some pastime from the dull hours of duty laid upon them.

As Jesus tugged at the cross to get on, He fell. The loss of blood and the weight of the beam had exhausted the human Christ. The whole grim procession came to a halt. Men stare, women weep, soldiers curse, and fellow criminals rest. In all this we behold a symbol of life with all its sordidness, hatred, and sin. However, Jesus is passing by and we behold the suffering Savior of mankind. What does all this mean to you and me?

I. SIMON OF CYRENE

In that crowd on the road to Calvary is one Simon, a Cyrenian. He had come to Jerusalem to observe the Passover. Little did Simon think as he munched at his morning meal, that later in the day, he would be forced to carry a cross after a criminal, who was to be crucified. He was an innocent bystander on the road, stopping to see what was happening. As this Jesus fell under His cross, the centurion looked about for some sturdy fellow whom he might draft into this service. His eyes fell on this Simon. Roman law permitted the centurion to call on anyone to render a service for the army or state if this chore did not take him more than two miles out of his way. So Simon became the "unfortunate" victim and was compelled and forced to carry the cross *after* Jesus. How his whole nature must have rebelled against this demand! He must obey orders and perform this to-him-distasteful job. And having done so, Simon stood on Calvary to see the end. That was truly a black Friday for him.

However, later in life, Simon was grateful that he had been chosen and compelled to carry the cross after Jesus. This tragic event became the crowning benediction in his life. No ... s given a greater distinction on that eventful day. But . moment, as Simon drags this cross up Calvary's hill resentment and bitterness is in his heart, lamenting the day that he happened along to be picked by that hated Roman officer.

Simon carried this burden under inward protest. The assignment came unexpectantly, seemingly, by chance. Had Simon lingered a little longer over his morning meal, he would have missed this procession, and the centurion never would have spotted him in that crowd. Undoubtedly Simon said in disgust: Why pick on me!

To Simon the task was without honor on that Friday morning. Having little knowledge of this Jesus, he saw in Him just another criminal. To be linked to such an evildoer, bore for him no honor. Simon felt himself humiliated. In his heart was resentment and defiance.

In the Afterglow

Yet in the *afterglow* of events this incident carried with it the mysterious. By this act of God's providence, Simon was *compelled* to go to Calvary and witness the crucifixion of Jesus. This must make us pause and ponder as we look back into some of our own yesteryears. We too have found ourselves confronted with some irksome task and our rebellious heart chafed under the sting of some handicap and humiliation, burdens not of our own making. God shut us in, deprived us of our most cherished pleasures and shattered our dreams. And our heart cried out for a God who cares. But as the days went on, we discovered that the unpleasant chore led us to Calvary, where we found healing from sin, peace of mind, and heaven.

In later years Simon discovered that the carrying of this

cross after Jesus was a most favorable discrimination shown him, or perchance any person in Christendom. Joseph of Arimathea and Nicodemus came later to honor Jesus in death and men and women admired them for their voluntary service offered at the close of the day, but Simon carried that ignoble cross after Jesus in the Galilean's deepest humiliation. So this forced service was the making of Simon. It riveted him to Christ. Only because of this act is Simon still remembered by the entire Christian world.

And what does this mean to us? We too are travelling the road to Calvary. This Jesus is inescapable to this very day. No matter where we are, what we are, what we do, we come face to face with this Jesus of Calvary. And He asks you and me to take up the cross and follow Him. As we do, much of the service carries with it no glamor. We are not going to stand in the limelight of applause if we boldly confess that we belong to Jesus who was crucified. And must we not admit, that we do not like to play second fiddle in the service of our Lord. Yet none of us Christians are spared the hardships of the Christian life. The world will stand against us if we stand up for Jesus. Too often we complain as we are confronted with such situations. Too many of us want an easy Christianity where there is no shedding of blood. However, the road to Calvary is laden with sacrifice and service, a complete surrender of our heart, our conscience, our will, and our lives.

But no matter how heavy the burden, how irksome the task, how humiliating the service rendered to Christ, it always has its compensations. Jesus makes every burden lighter. Jesus gives His recognition. Simon had the satisfaction to see his sons following in his footsteps in the service of Christ. They are active in the Jerusalem Church. His sons rose to call him blessed as they with him walked in the ways of the Lord.

As you and I travel the road to Calvary to behold the Savior die for us, let us, too, be ready to give each and every service to Jesus with a willing heart, even though no one recognizes and appreciates what we do among those who travel with us the road of life.

II. THE WEEPING WOMEN

In the crowd along the Way of Sorrows, the road to the cross, are a group of women whose sympathy has been awakened by the mere fact that a human being is suffering great distress. Their lament was against "man's inhumanity to man." As they bemoan Jesus' misfortune, He turns to them and says: "Weep not for Me!"

Was Jesus unappreciative of their sympathy? Had He become so callous that their lament left Him cold and indifferent? Hardly! Jesus Himself was so considerate and thoughtful. He went about doing good. Jesus loved people and healed them. He had invited all the weary and heavy laden to come to Him and find rest for their souls. Why, then, this rebuff as these women weep in sympathy, when Jesus falls under the weight of the cross?

These women did not realize that the One going to Calvary was more than a criminal. To them He was just another unfortunate human derelict who has been caught in the meshes of hatred and spite and brutality and could not escape. They saw the injustice of all, but there it ended.

Dare we stand by and look down our noses at these women? Are we any different? How often do we dismiss accounts of brutal injustice, crime, dishonesty, and inhuman treatment with the shrug of the shoulder and a sigh! "Too bad!" we say, "but what can we do?" We think we are meeting our obligation if we appear to be understanding, charitable in our judgment. Yet we leave all with the sigh and wish that things were different.

Jesus says that all this has little value. We must delve deeper into the matter. To the Jerusalem women Jesus points out that they too are a part of this sinful and sinning race of men. Therefore, they should look at themselves and weep over their own sins and shortcomings. Their transgressions, too, has made Calvary the altar of sacrifice, where the Lamb of God must die for sin, including theirs. However, His shedding of blood means nothing to them, unless they realize that their sins are crucifying the Lord of heaven and earth.

And this is our story, too. We have glamorized the cross on which Jesus died. Comfortably we are seated in our churches to hear the Passion of our Lord without ever a chill running down our spine, without ever contemplating the tremendous cost to the Son of God to redeem and save you and me. Jesus is looking for more than sympathizing tears. Christianity is more than a sentimental bouquet of wishful thinking. Jesus wants repentant hearts, which exclaim: "This awful death on Calvary was brought on by me and Jesus took my place that I might live, reconciled to God." His death alone gives me peace and hope and salvation. As we travel this road to Calvary, we must see more than another casualty of "man's inhumanity to man." We must behold the Lamb of God, taking our sins upon Himself that we may be restored to grace and find salvation.

III. THE TWO OTHER MALEFACTORS

Once more we look at the crowd on the road to Calvary and we see two other malefactors. Here are derelicts of humanity, the undesirables of skid row, who are a menace to human society and often dangerous to the community. They murder and kill, they steal and rob, they have no principles or morals. They belong to that segment of society of whom decent people are afraid and hope they will never meet in some lonely spot or some dark alley. They are the sore blotches of city and country. Jesus is led with them. He is classed with them by the leaders of Jerusalem as trouble makers who should be put out of the way. Are we shocked? Hardly, after the multitude has chosen Barabbas and demanded that Jesus be crucified. Men will stoop to anything to rid themselves of Jesus. He disturbs them.

How about us? You and I may not send Jesus to the gallows, but how often we banish him from our day and our lives. Jesus still disturbs. We are uncomfortable in His presence when we live in our sins. So we send Him away. We do not want Him around.

However, we must be made to realize that Jesus is numbered among transgressors, because He belongs there. God put Him there when He laid on Him our iniquities. As God sees Jesus with our sin on Him, God sees Him as the greatest of sinners, for upon Him is laid the sin of the *whole* world. This too we must understand, if the cross is to have any genuine significance for us, for you and me. Jesus never could have been numbered among transgressors and walked side by side with the two malefactors on the road to Calvary, if you and I had not sinned, sinned terribly and often. The Father pours out upon that Son the full wrath of His holiness that His justice and law might stand. Only because Jesus was the *sinless* Son of God could He bear our sins on that accursed tree and die to live again. His perfect sacrifice made a perfect atonement for us. That is why Jesus walks with the malefactors the road to Calvary.

None Past Redemption Point

Still more, Jesus is found walking with these malefactors that they might discover by the grace of God that even for them is hope. Men and women may stoop so low and wallow in the mire of the filthiest of sins and yet be cleansed and made whole and restored to grace. That is the glory of the Cross, that we need not close the door on any returning prodigal and say: This Gospel of the cross is not for you.

As Jesus walks side by side with these evildoers, He still loves them and does not want them to perish. And the one malefactor found this to be true. He heard on Calvary the most glorious promise ever given to a dying criminal. "Today —with Me—in Paradise." Because Jesus was led on that road to the cross with these two transgressors, each and every sinful soul can come and find cleansing and healing and heaven at the foot of the cross.

So the road of the cross is the road of sorrows. Along this way we see sin and death, suffering and pain, wickedness and crime, brutality and heartache, hatred and malice, shame and despair. However, on this road travels also One who comes with healing in His wings and makes us whole and into new creatures by His marvelous grace. We sinners become saints, we aliens become citizens, we slaves become children, we the disinherited become heirs. Amid all the sordidness of life stands Jesus who lifts us to His heart of love and washes away all that is ugly about us and clothes us in His holiness and gives us peace and hope, salvation and heaven.

> Oh wondrous love to bleed and die,
> To bear the cross and shame,
> That guilty sinners such as I
> Might plead Thy gracious Name!

2

THE PLACE OF THE CROSS

> *"And when they were come to the place,*
> *which is called Calvary, there they*
> *crucified Him."*—LUKE 23:33.

The place where Jesus was crucified is called Calvary in Greek; Golgotha in Hebrew; The Skulls in English. The place had this name even before Jesus was nailed to the accursed tree. The site is unknown to modern time and therefore we cannot say *why* the mount was designated as The Skulls. At the present two places contend for the distinction. The one is in the Church of the Holy Sepulchre and is called the Chapel of Calvary. The other is just outside of the present Damascus Gate of Jerusalem and is known as Gordon's Calvary. We ask: How could a place of such importance be lost to the memory of man? The answer: During the persecutions of the early church Christians were not permitted to dwell in nor come to Jerusalem. During that period even an attempt was made to build a Jupiter Temple on the Temple site. Not until the days of Constantine were Christians permitted to come to the Jewish Capital. This was about three hundred years after the crucifixion. By this time no one who came to the holy city or lived there knew the place where Jesus was crucified.

Little importance need to be attached to the *where* of Calvary. Of utmost significance and far-reaching in effect for you and me is to know *what* took place on Calvary. *"There they crucified Him."*

I. CALVARY—WHERE SIN DOES ITS WORST

The place of the cross is called Calvary. There sin does its

worst. The glaring spotlight is thrown on sin and its destructive power. We see sin in its stark ugliness. Sin is so terrible
that it crucified and killed the Son of God, in whom was no
sin. That which nailed Jesus to the tree was *our* iniquity
which was laid on Him. As we behold Him suffer and die on
Golgotha we discover the horrible reality of sin. Standing
beneath that cross we see for ourselves how much we have
missed the mark and how utterly we have failed to do the will
of God. Only because our transgressions were laid on Him
could all these things be done to Him as the Lamb of God
which takes away the sin of the world. As the searchlight is
focused on that Central Figure we cannot fail to note how
hideous, how cruel, how black, how damning sin can be.
Here on Calvary we are made to realize at what tremendous
price we sinners have been redeemed and released from the
clutches of Satan. Only through the death of the Son of God
could we be set free with the joy of forgiveness in our hearts.
The greater the price paid, the more should we appreciate
and value our deliverance.

Think of the sacrifices in blood and life, property and
money, which has been made that we might enjoy liberty, a
freedom only for this world! In the early history of the Swiss
people Arnold von Winkelrid is supposed to have given his
life that the Swiss might remain a free nation. As the story
is told the Austrians made war on the people and were march-
ing forward ruthlessly taking everything which came their
way. No matter what the Swiss army did, it could not break
through and stop the oncoming opponents. It was then that
Winkelrid stepped forward—so the story runs—rushed ahead
alone, as he commended his own family into the hands of
his fellow soldiers. As the Austrians saw him coming on, they
threw their spears at him and into his body. Dead he fell to
the ground. But at that place an opening was made where
the Swiss could rush in for the Austrian spears were all in the
body of the lifeless Winkelrid. So he gave his life to keep
Switzerland free. However, on Golgotha's cross through the

death of *one* we have been given a freedom and a deliverance which saved our souls from the serfdom of Satan and the hell of eternity and made us acceptable to God. As we view this Jesus, forsaken of God, in the pangs of damnation, we must come to the full realization of the perilous plight of us sinners and the destructive power of our disobedience. Sin separates us from God. Sin sends us to eternal damnation from which there is no escape. This we must realize. On Calvary sin does its worst, for there the Son of God pays the *full* price of our redemption.

II. CALVARY—WHERE LOVE IS AT ITS BEST

The place of the cross is called Calvary. There we see love at its best. As Jesus is nailed to that tree of humiliation, despised and rejected of man, the milling crowd, goaded on by the Jerusalem leaders, challenges Jesus to come down from the cross. "If Thou be the Son of God, come down from the cross" (Matthew 27:40). Even one of the malefactors screams at Him: "If Thou be the Christ, save Thyself and us." Little did he realize that Jesus was doing just that, paying for this criminal's sins which had brought him to this horrible death.

Why did Jesus not come down from the cross and meet this challenge? Certainly this would have been a convincing evidence of His divine sonship! What more startling and impressive demonstration that He was more than a carpenter's son! Surely the nails did not hold Him powerless to the beam when at other times winds and waves obeyed Him. As the Almighty He could have stepped down, called upon hundreds of angels to smite down the taunting mob. Why did Jesus not do so? What held Him to that cross? *Love,* love for you and me and for those who crucified Him.

Had Jesus come down, the throng would have been overawed, and then would have burst forth into a hilarious acceptance of Him as a wonderman. But if He had come down, you and I would still be in the hands of Satan and sin, lost and condemned creatures. *Love* held Jesus to that cross, that

He might pay the full price of our redemption and be crowned King of eternity and Savior of all mankind. Because He remained on that cross to pay the total ransom price for sin, you and I are sure of our salvation. In the Upper Room Jesus had announced: "Greater love hath no man than this, that a man lay down his life for his friends" (John 15:13). This supreme love held Jesus to the cross. There never was love like this!

David left Jerusalem, ready to give up his throne with all its glory because of his love for Absalom, his son. Even after Absalom came to his ignoble death, we hear the father exclaim: "Would to God that I had died for thee! O Absalom, my son, my son!" But David could not give his life to redeem his son.

Ruth gave up her homeland for the love she had for Naomi and the faith that was in her mother-in-law who had witnessed a good confession in the land of Moab. Ruth gained much *for herself* by coming to Bethlehem. But her love and devotion to Naomi and her faithfulness to God does not help you and me out of our sins and the fear of death.

Jesus remained on that cross that you and I may find forgiveness and peace. While we were in sin, unlovable and spiteful, Christ died for us. Only because Jesus loved us so, remained on that cross on that Friday, gave His life, is heaven opened to you and me and our eternal home. So we see *love* at its best on Calvary's cross.

III. CALVARY—WHERE FORSAKENNESS REACHES A NEW LOW

The place of the cross is called Calvary. There forsakenness reaches a new low.

Jesus is forsaken by His followers. Judas betrayed Him for the paltry thirty pieces of silver. That money could not even buy him a good farm. In the garden all the other disciples fled and were scattered to the winds. Even boasting Peter followed from afar and soon lost courage as he warmed himself at the patio fires. Then he altogether denied his Lord, covering his identity with cursing and swearing. Simon's boast in the Upper Room seemed mighty hollow at the enemies' brazier: "I will lay down my life for Thy sake" (John 13: 37).

But dare *we* point the finger of scorn at Peter? Have we not too often hid our identity by aping the world in which we live and move? Do we ever speak to the man on the assembly line of the hope that is in us? Are we only interested in getting much work out of the office staff, never asking: What about their souls? Time and again, you and I forsake Him who hangs there on Calvary. And His heart breaks as you and I go away.

Jesus is forsaken by the multitude. That numberless people on Calvary is made up of every type of humanity. Look into their faces! Are you astonished that they look so much like yourself! And what is this surging mob doing? Some are gambling at the foot of the cross; others are sneering, mocking, jesting. Nothing kind is said. "Himself He cannot save!" "Come down from the cross, if you can!" "Build the Temple in three days, you boaster!"

Down the ages humanity forsakes this Jesus; and for what? For the pleasures of sin, for the diamond mines of Golconda, for the lust of power, for the smiles of the world. We make ourselves into gods. Even at this moment many deny, betray, hide from Jesus, mock at Christianity. The cross is foolishness still to many. Pride, self-righteousness, conceit stand between Christ and millions. And yet He hangs there, died there, that you and I and all may be without excuse. Jesus pleads: "Come, come to Me. I will give rest to your souls."

Forsaken of God

Jesus is forsaken of God. Yes, God pours out upon Him the complete judgment for sin and turns His face from His beloved Son. That is what Scripture says. On that cross is heard the heart-cry of the Son of God: "My God, My God,

why hast Thou forsaken Me?" Forsaken! Can you imagine
the depth of this word? Hardly!

You and I have never been forsaken by God, even though
some of our friends have turned against us. Even in the utmost misery, the most distressing heartaches, complete loss of
all possessions, we still live and have our being. God has not
forsaken us. God may not give us all that we want. We may
feel so alone in our distress and face a very unfriendly world,
but God still is with us. In this world it is not possible to be
completely and altogether forsaken of God. There is only one
place where we can and are totally separated from the Lord
of heaven and earth—that is in hell. That is where Jesus was
when He cried out: "Eli, Eli! Why hast Thou forsaken Me?"
Jesus was suffering the pangs of hell and the damned.

Yet in hell He prayed, "My God!" He turned not from His
God, but clung to Him. Therein lies our salvation. Jesus
suffered forsakenness that the justice of the Law of God be
completely satisfied. Knowing this, that Jesus on Calvary made
complete atonement for sin, our conscience can be at ease.
We have a perfect Savior from sin, because in that dark hour
forsakenness reached a new low.

IV. CALVARY—WHERE VICTORY CLIMBS TO A NEW HIGH

The place of the cross is called Calvary. There victory
climbed to a new high. The greatest battle of the ages was
fought here and Jesus *won*.

Many important battles have been fought in the history of
the world. At Marathon a decisive battle was fought which
saved Greece and all western civilization; at Waterloo Europe
wrestled itself from a complete subjection to Napoleon; at
Saratoga the battle decided the independence of America.
Even during our lifetime important battles have been fought,
which have changed the maps of the world and the outlook
of man. However, all these fade into insignificance with the
Battle of Calvary. There Jesus won the victory over Satan

and emancipated man from the guilt of sin and the fear of death and the judgment to come. There on the cross Jesus assured salvation for all sinners. Now we stand beneath that cross by faith and are promised with the dying thief heaven with all its glory. And this is final. "There is no condemnation to them which are in Christ Jesus" (Romans 8:1). With Paul each believer can exclaim: "I have fought a good fight, I have finished my course, I have kept the faith: Henceforth there is laid up for me a crown of righteousness, which the Lord, the righteous Judge, shall give me at that day; and not to me only, but unto all them also that love His appearing" (2 Timothy 4:7, 8).

But more—our old Adam—this sinful nature of ours was taken to the cross and died in and with Christ. On that cross our victory is sure. "If the Son therefore shall make you free, ye shall be free indeed" (John 8:36). So Calvary is the one and only place where we can win spiritual victories. Victory climbs to a new high on Calvary.

V. ON CALVARY REBORN BY FAITH

The place of the cross is called Calvary. There we are made into new creatures by faith in Him who was crucified for us. Being reborn we pledge new allegiance to Him as our King and we serve Him as our Lord. We live in His kingdom as citizens of a new world and are of the household, children of His grace and heirs of eternal life.

Thus Jesus who on Calvary wears the crown of thorns no longer wears it in humiliation and shame. Through the cross that crown becomes the insignia of triumph. Jesus is now the King of the ages. He is the Savior of all believers from century to century and our triumphant King throughout eternity.

Truly, this Calvary is the most sacred place in all the world! Here the Lamb of God takes away the sin of the world and washes, cleanses, heals us, and restores to grace all who stand beneath the cross. And in heaven these believers, washed white in the blood of the Lamb, sing the new song of eternity: "Thou wast slain, and hast redeemed us to God by Thy blood out of every kindred, and tongue, and people, and nation; and hast made us unto our God kings and priests" (Revelation 5:9, 10). Hallelujah! Amen.

3

THE INSCRIPTION OF THE CROSS

> *"And Pilate wrote a title, and put it on the cross. And the writing was,* JESUS OF NAZARETH THE KING OF THE JEWS. *This title then read many of the Jews; for the place where Jesus was crucified was nigh to the city: and it was written in Hebrew, and Greek, and Latin. Then said the chief priests of the Jews to Pilate, Write not, The King of the Jews; but that He said, I am King of the Jews. Pilate answered, What I have written I have written."*
> —John 19:19-22.

Pontius Pilate wrote a superscription which was nailed to the cross. This plaque was to tell the people of the Passover week *who* He was who hung on that central cross and *what* crime He had committed and been found guilty. Pilate seemingly wrote this inscription himself: Jesus of Nazareth, the King of the Jews. The Jerusalem leaders objected to the wording. They did not want it said that Jesus *was* King of the Jews. Such a statement might incriminate them and they definitely repudiated such a claim. However, Pontius Pilate for once held his ground and said: "What I have written I have written." He refused to budge. But methinks that this is not the whole story. God wanted this to be the wording and have that stand. However, Pontius Pilate said more than he realized, for Jesus *is* King. So the inscription stood and was nailed to the cross.

The statement was written in Hebrew and Greek and Latin. These were the three major languages of the Roman Empire. Everyone at Jerusalem most likely could read at least one or two of the three. Pontius Pilate wanted to make sure that everyone knew on what charge Jesus of Nazareth was crucified.

I. IN HEBREW—FOR THE ETHICAL WORLD

Hebrew was the language of God's people of the Old Testament age. God revealed Himself in the Hebrew in the days before Jesus. It was the language spoken by Moses and the prophets. Through this language God made known His holy will on Sinai and His gracious will through the promises of the coming Messiah. Amid the idolatrous people of ancient days God intoned to Israel: "Hear, O Israel, the Lord our God is *one* Lord. And thou shalt love the Lord thy God with all thine heart, and with all thy soul, and with all thy might. And these words, which I command thee this day, shall be in thine heart" (Deuteronomy 6:4-6).

The Hebrew people accepted Jehovah, who had given His name at the Burning Bush, Exodus 3:14, and had spoken His holy will on Sinai, Exodus 20. To Israel God was self-evident. Even the heavens declare the glory of God, and therefore all mankind, except the fool, knows that there is a God. But God's will, the highest moral and spiritual values, God must make known to mankind by revelation. This God has done in the Holy Scriptures. So the *heart* must be turned to God, the *heart* which is natively wicked, uncontrolled, rebellious. As long as the *heart* runs amuck, the world will ignore and defy God. Even many will say: There is no God.

Since the Hebrew people accepted Jehovah as God and were guided and directed in their thoughts and lives by the revealed precepts of the Lord, they stood out from the nations of the ancient world as a unique people. In their worship they acknowledged and confessed only *one* God and made no graven images to which they bowed down. In their home life they reared their children in the fear of the Lord. Their moral and ethical standards were much higher than that of the Gentiles. Foremost to the observation of the world around them was the Israelite's practice of monogamy, having one wife. Because of the higher standard prevailing in Israel, many of them became self-righteous and thought their outward obedience to the Law of God entitled them to salvation.

"Give Me Your Heart"

To these morally more acceptable people was written in Hebrew, their worship and prayer language: This Jesus is King. Jesus claims the *heart*. He asks for our love, our devotion, our allegiance, our service. We are to apply ourselves earnestly to the doing of the will of God, walk uprightly, "be good". And why? Because He first loved us and gave His life for our redemption. Jesus must have the right of way to our lives and dwell in us as Savior, who cleanses our hearts and makes them temples of His indwelling. Only then will we worship Him as our Lord and God and King, who has purchased us with His life-blood to be His own.

Many religious people of the twentieth century reject this kind of a Jesus. They are ready to accept Him as the Ideal, the Perfect Character, the Wayshower. But sin is outmoded and relegated to the past with goblins and witches and ghosts. Modern religionists want no Savior from sin. Even though terribly afraid of the future their anxieties have to do with world destruction of our fellowmen. They want a Savior from bombs and missiles. They want a security for this world. The Christ of Calvary belongs to history of the past.

But Jesus will not be bowed out. *The cross still stands.* What was written 1900 years ago still is written: Jesus *is* King and Lord. This statement of Pilate is unalterably true, not because Pilate wrote it, but because God says: "This *is* My beloved Son!" There is no other Way to life eternal; there is no other Name under heaven whereby mankind can be saved. "No man cometh unto the Father, *but by Me,*" says Jesus. No one is at peace with God, no one has a good conscience, no one has any permanent hope, no one is certain and sure of salvation until he acclaims Jesus the Savior of his soul and

King of his heart. To the ethical and religious world the cross with this *Hebrew* inscription proclaims: Jesus alone saves.

II. IN GREEK—FOR THE INTELLECTUAL WORLD

Greek was the language of the intellectual and cultural world. The arts and the philosophies of the ancients came chiefly from the Greeks. Greek was the universal language of the Roman Empire. Most people were bilingual. They spoke their native tongue and Greek. The Greek people had given the world the magnificent Parthenon on the Acropolis in Athens. The Greeks had given the world the basic principles of logic, drama, mathematics, medicine. The Greeks gave the world Aristotle, Socrates, Plato, and many others.

The Greek people appealed to the *mind*. Everything must be perceived through the five senses. Man's wisdom was exalted above all as the greatest achievement in the world. Our Western civilization is built upon this Greek foundation in the arts, in science, in philosophy, in physics. Our culture is basically Greek in pattern and we are not ashamed to admit this.

God used the Greek language to pen the New Testament Scriptures. This greatest of all documents of the world, which tells us *how* we are saved, namely through faith in Christ Jesus, was written in *Greek*.

Greek thought and Greek philosophy gave man no hope for the world to come. At Athens the wise snickered when Paul addressed them on Mars' Hill on the Resurrection. This seemed foolishness to them. So they laughed him out of town, calling him a babbler or chatterer. The Greeks made their appeal to the *mind* and refused to accept practically all that could not be perceived through the five senses and logically demonstrated.

To this "Greek" *mind* the inscription of the cross announced that Jesus *is* King. Jesus claims this realm also for Himself. No one can think straight, think thoughts after

God, unless Jesus is at the heart and center of his thinking. The mind and the intellect cannot find the way to God. With all the intelligence the Greek philosophers possessed, they did not find God. Jehovah was unknown to them. As Paul walked up Mars' Hill he saw more than a thousand altars along the way. Even an altar to the *Unknown God* had been erected. Man's intellect is so blinded to that which is spiritual that without the revelations of God, he cannot find and know Jehovah and His Son, Jesus Christ, as Savior from sin.

The Modern Mind and Christ

Modern thought and philosophy, based on Greek culture and learning, has to a large extent rejected Jesus as the Savior of humanity. True, nominally we speak of ourselves as a Christian nation. We cannot deny that the Jesus influence is evident in all places. We have inscribed even on our coins the words: "In God we trust." However, we smile at the beatitudes as impracticable and the Golden Rule as an idealistic motto, which must not be taken too seriously. The modern world, as of old, glorifies its own self as self-sufficient. We boast of space travel and coming moon vacations and point with pride at our technical accomplishments. Such a world does not want to come to the cross and confess shortcomings and sins and ask for forgiveness. Sin is merely a struggle upward and surely none should be faulted for being ambitious. Therefore, the wisdom of the world does not want Jesus as King. The modern *mind* places success ahead of moral goodness. Moral standards are flexible codes of vacillating public opinions. So the world goes ahead feverishly in its technical drive and builds more and better gadgets but lags behind in its moral attainments. Glorious as such a life may seem, the soul is not satisfied. Fattened oxen and filled barns do not put the *mind* at ease.

To such a restless, feverish, and aggravated world Jesus comes and says that only *He* can put the *mind* at ease and give that peace which the world cannot give. Without Him the most brilliant *mind* becomes self-centered, selfish, brutal, and destructive. We have better machinery, better homes, better travelling facilities—yet are filled with fear, hopelessness, and are inhuman to humans. If Christ Jesus does not become the center of our thinking, we shall destroy ourselves and our civilization.

All this lies behind the words: It is written in Greek.

III. IN LATIN—FOR THE POWERS THAT BE

Latin was the official language of the Roman Government. Pilate himself spoke Latin, as he brought Jesus out on the Pavement or Gabbatha, saying to the howling mob. "Ecce Homo!—Behold the Man!"

To the powers that be, Jesus, by contrast, is the King of love. Rome ruled the world with an iron hand. Mercy and clemency were not written into the law of the land. Rome's power was built upon force. The state was supreme at all times. What Rome said was law. The Empire stood like the Rock of Gibraltar as long as the standing army could maintain order and compel obedience to the law. All opposition to the state was crushed with ruthless severity. Rome knew too well that, if a stronger army would come, the Empire would collapse. Therefore, the standing army could be rushed over the well-kept roads of the Empire to any part of the Mediterranean world to quell any uprising and subdue the conquered nation into obedience.

It has always been so that might is right in the history of the nations. Nebucadnezzar, Alexander, Julius Caesar, Genghis Khan, Tamerlane, Napoleon and many others founded their empires on force. The mightiest survived. Such kingdoms, however, eventually crumbled.

Latin stands for this kind of power. The law of the state is final and all who stand in the way are trampled under foot. The Emperor and the hero are worshipped and feared and the individual must be sacrificed for the so-called "general good" of state. That is the thinking of the powers that be.

THE INSCRIPTION OF THE CROSS 33

The Kingdom of Love

To these powers comes Jesus and says: "My kingdom is not of this world; if My kingdom were of this world, then would My servants fight, that I should not be delivered to the Jews" (John 18:36). Yet Jesus claimed power such as none of the rulers of the world have. Said Jesus to Pilate: "Thou couldest have no power at all against Me, except it were given thee from above" (John 19:11). Jesus claims that His kingdom is an everlasting kingdom against which the gates of hell shall not be able to prevail. However, His kingdom is built upon sacrifice, forgiveness, mercy, *love*. Jesus governs the world of men by seeing in them more than a number in the index files. He sees in them persons, individuals, to be loved and saved. He is interested in the spiritual values of man. Therefore He says: "What shall it profit a man, if he shall gain the whole world, and lose his own soul?" (Mark 8:36). Even Alexander, who wept that there were no more worlds to conquer, did not realize how small a part of the earth he had embodied in his kingdom. Jesus puts the greatest value on the souls and, therefore, became flesh and laid down His life to save us from the kingdom of darkness and makes us citizens of heaven.

Modern government to a large extent ignores Christ and His teachings of love. They want none of it. Jesus is bypassed in the corridors of the nations. One nation must outdo the other, and power and force, armies and navies, bombs and missiles are of greater importance than individual lives and the gospel of the Crucified, who alone saves man from eternal destruction.

Yet on that cross the powers that be are told: Jesus *is* King and His kingdom is an everlasting kingdom. In vain do the nations plot, scheme, deride the thorn-crowned Jesus of Nazareth. To the rulers of the world whose political ambitions often make them ruthless and heartless, God already says in David's day: "I will declare the decree: the Lord hath said unto Me, Thou art My Son; this day have I begotten Thee. Ask of Me, and I shall give Thee the heathen for Thine inheritance, and the uttermost parts of the earth for Thy possession. Thou shalt break them with a rod of iron; Thou shalt dash them in pieces like a potter's vessel. Be wise now therefore, O ye kings: be instructed, ye judges of the earth. Serve the Lord with fear, and rejoice with trembling. Kiss the Son, lest He be angry, and ye perish from the way, when His wrath is kindled but a little. Blessed are all they that put their trust in Him" (Psalm 2:7-12) .

The *will* of man must accept Jesus. Man cannot go his own *willful* way and succeed. Jesus must guide and direct our lives and *our will*, lest we beat out our heads against the wall of stubbornness and go to destruction eternally.

All this lies behind the words: It is written in Latin.

It is written in Hebrew, Greek, and Latin; it is written in all languages of the world: Jesus *is* King. To the *heart*, to the *mind*, to the *will* is said: *Jesus is King.* To the Gentiles and the Jews, to the Greek and the Barbarian, to the freeman and to the slave, to all, the cross proclaims *Jesus is King and Savior.* That is why He gives His life that we might have a hope and a heaven.

This thorn-crowned King-Savior knocks at the door of our hearts and wants to enter in and take full possession of our mind and will and give us that peace which the world cannot give. In Him we find a joy that is complete and a heaven that is eternal.

> Let every kindred, every tribe
> On this terrestrial ball
> To Him all majesty ascribe
> *And crown Him Lord of all.*

4

THE PLEDGE OF THE CROSS

> *"When Jesus therefore had received the vinegar,*
> *He said: It is finished."*—John 19:30
> *"And Jesus said unto him, Verily I say unto thee,*
> *Today shalt thou be with Me in Paradise."*—Luke 23:43.

The Bible is a casebook of repentance and brings hope to each and every soul in distress. This truth is emphasized on Calvary's cross, where the Savior of man takes upon Himself the sins of the world and *pledges* and underwrites salvation for all mankind. As Jesus is nailed to the cross, He prays: Father, forgive them. Forgive all sins to all sinners; the worst sinner and the most degenerate sinner. Is this possible? Is this practicable? It must be, if Jesus is the Lamb of God who takes away the sin of the world.

During His public ministry, Jesus invited people from all walks and conditions of life to seek Him in their distress, saying: "Come unto Me, all ye that labor and are heavy laden . . . and ye shall find rest unto your souls" (Matthew 11:28, 29). And then Jesus promises: "Him that cometh to Me, I will in no wise cast out" (John 6:37). *That is the pledge of the cross.* This pledge Jesus makes to the sinner, because of the other pledge, which He made on Calvary's cross, when He exclaimed: *It is finished.* This pledge to the thief, "Today . . . with Me . . . in Paradise," has value only, because Jesus completed the work of redemption, which He announces to heaven, earth, and hell, as He calls out with a loud voice: *Finished!*

I. THE FIRST PLEDGE

"It is finished!" With these words Jesus announces to the

world that the reconciliation between God and man has been accomplished. Jesus went to the altar of the cross to be sacrificed as the Lamb of God. With the shedding of His blood, Jesus was to pay the price of our redemption. Isaiah had foretold: "He was wounded for our transgressions, He was bruised for our iniquities; the chastisement of our peace was upon Him; and with His stripes we are healed" (Isaiah 53:5). Therefore John the Baptist, seeing this Jesus for the first time, pointed to Him with the words: "Behold the Lamb of God, which taketh away the sin of the world" (John 1:29). The blood sacrifice was to be the ransom price to be paid to release us from the power of sin.

Jesus could do this because He was the sinless Son of God. None other was and is capable of accomplishing this heroic deed which would pay the full price of redemption. The Psalmist already knew this as he states in Psalm 49: "None of them can by any means redeem his brother, nor give to God a ransom for him, for the redemption of their soul is precious, and it ceaseth forever." "For the ransom of his life is costly, and can never suffice" (RSV). Man through the ages has tried to redeem himself but failed. Savage tribes have cut deep gashes into their cheeks, devotees of India have slept on beds of spiked nails, pagans of Carthage have offered human sacrifices to Moloch, Flagellentes have beaten their bare backs until they fell exhausted to the ground from loss of blood. But no matter what man does, his accomplishments and tortures still leave him a sinner. His accusing conscience tells his distressed soul, that he does not enough to appease and satisfy the justice of God.

God must step in and make a way of escape from the powers of darkness which hold humanity shackled and imprisoned in sin. God laid on His Son the iniquity of all sinners and sent Him to the cross of Calvary as the divine Lamb of God to shed His blood and die to make good for the sin of the world. On Calvary Jesus went to the fortresses of hell and fought the powers of darkness *and won*. "It is finished!" is the cry of victory. This is the guarantee and the pledge that the task is *done* and the battle is over.

And what does this mean to you and me? For one thing—the guilt of sin and the curse of the Law is removed from us. The Sinai Commandments cannot demand judgment against us who stand beneath the cross. Through the shedding of His blood remission of sin is guaranteed.

The cross establishes through this pledge a second fact: Death has lost its sting. Death cannot hold mankind in the grave. "The hour is coming, in the which all that are in the graves shall hear His voice, And shall come forth; They that have done good, unto the resurrection of life; and they that have done evil, unto the resurrection of damnation" (John 5:28, 29). Man can go into death via the cross and sleep to rise to life everlasting.

The third fact which is established through this victory is this that Satan and his ilk can be resisted. The believer has the power through this cross to stand up against the temptations of the devil and say No. "Get thee hence, Satan!"—and out he must go.

This is the pledge of the cross: Salvation *is* finished. It is an accomplished fact. God *is* reconciled to the sinner. The Way is done. And it is a *sure way*, but the only Way. "No man cometh unto the Father, *but by me*" (John 14:6).

II. THE PLAN WORKS

The pledge is made. The guarantee is given. "It is finished!" Salvation *is* an accomplished fact. A salvation is there for all sinners. Is this really true? Is such a plan workable in a world of sin? Can the redemption of the cross save to the uttermost? The plan is tried at once. A man, hopelessly lost in sin and in the throes of death and at the brink of hell, turns to Jesus for help. As he does, he is given the most glorious promise that can be given to any human soul faced with the damnation of hell: "Today thou shalt be with Me in Paradise."

To whom is this pledge made? To the one thief, hanging

and dying on the cross. This thief makes an honest confession. He admits that the trial was fair and the verdict of guilt just. He was receiving the due reward of his deeds. He makes no complaint nor does he try to hide behind some alibi. He acknowledges his guilt and says that he deserves every bit of that punishment meted out to him that day.

He admits more: That there is a future life, for this Man on the central cross has a kingdom in another world. In that eternity man meets his Master, and justice is carried out. Man does not only pay for his sins in *this* world, but also in the courts of God. As the thief thinks on these things and of the trial in God's courts, he confesses his utter helplessness to escape. However, He believes that he has *one* chance: He is convinced in his own heart that this Jesus of Nazareth can and will do something for him.

A Declaration of Belief

Four statements the thief makes concerning this Nazarene, King of the Jews. He has done nothing amiss. This Jesus is without guilt. He can stand in the courts of His eternal Father and need not plead forgiveness. This Jesus has fulfilled the will and the law of the Eternal. Sinai cannot condemn Him. Secondly, the thief believes that this Jesus is Lord. So he addresses Him who hangs on that central cross. He uses the Greek name for Jehovah. To him Jesus is more than a prophet, more than the ideal character. To him Jesus is God. So he addresses Jesus as Lord-Jehovah. Thirdly, the thief is certain that this Jesus has a salvation to give. He *has* a kingdom. And in that kingdom is an escape from all the torture of body, conscience, and soul. In that kingdom is healing from the guilt and the escape from the curse of sin. There sin has no power over the souls of man. And finally—and this is most important to the thief—he believes that this salvation is *for him*. Believing this the malefactor turns to this Jesus on the central tree and pleads: "Lord, remember me, when Thou comest into Thy kingdom."

Seeking Help at the Right Place

This thief, let us note with emphasis, went for refuge and for help to the right place. In his utmost distress he realized that there was no other escape. He was convinced that the Law of God could not help him. He is past that stage, for he knows that he has sinned too much and too often to appeal to the Law and seek and find refuge and exhonoration there. He has no chance to stand on his good record. As he pleads for help, he does not ask to be taken down from the cross and given another chance in this world. He has made a mess of this life and knows very well that even to try to do better would be of no avail. He is willing to take the full payment for sin in this world. All he asks is an escape from the damnation of eternity. For this liberation he depends solely and alone on the mercies of Him who is dying at the same time with him on Calvary.

At this point we want to state that this Calvary is the *one* place where you and I must go, if we want to have any hope of salvation. No matter who you are, you *with me* must come to this Jesus to be saved. To live in this grace wherein we stand we must be washed, cleansed, and healed daily. No matter *how good* you are, how respected in the community because of your fine conduct, how noble in character, you still must come to the cross to be saved. If you and I are honest with ourselves, we must admit with John the Apostle, one of the saintliest among men: "If we say that we have no sin, we deceive ourselves and the truth is not in us." Not one of us can stand in God's presence and say: I have at no time broken Thy Law of Sinai! We all, one by one, must come for the healing of our souls to the cross of Jesus, where His blood cleanseth us from all sin.

On the other hand, we too can say, and this is Gospel truth, no matter how wicked a person has been, a degenerate and outcast of society, a sinner of the deepest dye, he can come to Jesus and He will not close the door upon him and say: "Not wanted." Jesus makes the foulest clean. This is why David could come and the Lord created in him a clean heart. That is why Paul found peace of heart and mind, even though he admits that he was the greatest of sinners. That is why Simon Peter could come and be restored to grace. "Him that cometh unto Me, I will in no wise cast out." So says Jesus.

That is the pledge of Him who exclaimed on Calvary with a triumphant voice: "It is finished!"

III. THE SECOND PLEDGE OF THE CROSS

To that thief, pleading for mercy and help in his utmost extremities, the compassionate Savior gives a pledge and a promise: "Verily, I say unto thee, Today shalt thou be with Me in Paradise." We see here the height of compassion. For years Jesus had been going about doing good. The sick were healed, the troubled helped, the blind were given sight, the sorrowing comforted, the distressed helped. None came to Him in vain. However, Jesus' tenderness reached a new high on the cross as He saved the thief in the eleventh hour of his life. Seemingly there was little difference between the two, Jesus and the thief. Both had been condemned to death by crucifixion and were suffering alike, pain, thirst, shame, humiliation. Yet between them was a vast difference. The one was helpless and the other a Savior. The one was receiving the due penalties of justice for sins confessed, the Other is suffering for the sins of the thief and the world. To this evildoer who pleads for help Jesus pledges Paradise. None could have a greater Friend! Only God could show this kind of pity! Only the compassion of God could do something definitely for this man in his hopeless plight. And Jesus is that God who helps. You and I often sympathize with people in their sorrow and distress, but are just as helpless as they. We can do nothing to relieve them. But Jesus has the ability and the willingness to lift the thief out of the mess in which he finds himself. *Jesus* could do this, and He only, because He is Jehovah-God. He can save to the uttermost and in the extremities of life. At the brink of hell Jesus could rescue the malefactor, by paying in full the total penalty which the just and holy and righteous God demands in His displeasure of sin. Nothing like this is to be found anywhere in heaven and on earth. This divine Savior could pledge Paradise because He had finished the redemption on the cross.

This is Gospel. This is glad news today, for Jesus still has the power to save you and me for Paradise. This pledge guarantees the giving to and the sharing of Paradise with Him to all who come to the cross.

What is Paradise?

Paradise is the home of God, where angels and saints abide in the presence of the Lamb, who has redeemed us with His own blood. The redeemed of heaven sing praises to Him who has given us Paradise. In that glory is fullness of joy, a final and continued bliss. In this present world no joy is lasting or complete. Today we are happy as a lark and tomorrow sorrowful unto death. Sickness and pain burden our day; heartaches and disappointments take the sunshine out of our hearts; failures and setbacks embitter our lives; and old age and feebleness fill our day with insecurity and worry. In Paradise God shall wipe away all tears from our eyes and there shall be no more pain. And why? Because we shall be like Him who went to the cross to make us heirs of all that is eternal. This Paradise is His everlasting kingdom. Death has no place there. We shall live forever in that glory. That is the pledge of our Savior.

Having this blessed assurance and our eternal destiny secured we believers already in this world, even amid the tribulations of life, have that *peace* which passeth understanding, and that *hope* which never fades nor fails. Our salvation is guaranteed through this pledge which opens the way to the very heart of God.

To this day Jesus turns to each and every sinner who comes pleading for mercy and for forgiveness and promises: "Today

shalt thou be with Me in Paradise." He is eager and anxious
to save you and me, and *all* sinners. He sees in you and me
souls that He must save if we are to be saved and find Paradise our eternal home. This pledge of salvation, therefore,
Jesus underwrites with an oath to make it doubly binding:
"Verily, I say unto thee." We know of a certainty that His
promises never fail.

However, as we stand in spirit on Calvary's brow and see
Jesus hanging on that accursed tree to make certain our salvation, what are *we* doing? Are we shooting dice with the
soldiers? Are we so concerned about getting things that are
perishable and temporal that we take no time out to look up to
Him whose outstretched arms plead with us to come? Are
money, fine clothes, popularity, success more important to us
than Paradise? Are we passing by and sneering: Come down,
and give us health and wealth and prestige? Is it so important
to us that we get all we can out of this present world and take
a chance at Paradise? Or are we with the dying thief and all
believers turning to Him with the penitent plea of a devoted
and consecrated heart, saying: Lord, remember me! Lord, keep
me in Thy grace and love till journey's end! If so, then this
Jesus will give to us, too, the blessed pledge and guaranteed
promise: "With Me"—verily—"in Paradise."

5

THE ENEMIES OF THE CROSS

"For many walk, of whom I have told you often, and now tell you even weeping, that they are the enemies of the cross of Christ."—Philippians 3:18.

The world of men and nations has been in a perpetual upheaval through the centuries. Things were certainly a mess at Jerusalem that last Passover which Jesus attended. Nationalism ran high in defiance of the Roman yoke which gave Israel's holy city Pontius Pilate as governor. The eye of every Jew registered resentment at the presence of the Roman legions. Therefore, the Roman state sent re-enforcements to the city for the Passover week, ready for any emergency. Riots and fightings were the order of the day. The Romans even built a tower overlooking the Temple site so that the captain might have a bird's eye view of the milling crowd and dispatch soldiers down into the courts to disperse the disturbers. Agitators against Roman rule, isolationists of every stripe kept the seething pot boiling. Besides this the people fought, quarreled, argued among themselves. Some were Herodians, others Sadducees, some zealots. Discrimination against the Samaritans and suspicion as to the loyalty of the Galileans added fuel to the fire. Hatred, spite, trickery, jealousy, brutality, cruelty, vengeance made up the long roster of hostilities. Everyone was against some one. Some person or group had to be hated to give vent to pent-up emotions.

Into the center of this varicolor mass of people, vicious with emotions, unshackled violence and defiance *God sets that cross on Calvary*. At once and with concerted accord these evil forces unite in their opposition to Him who hangs on that central, accursed tree.

What has He done? Why—He made their blind see; He
cleansed their lepers; He fed them by the thousands. He went
about healing those who were physically sick, mentally disturbed, branded and bruised by sin. He loved them, sympa-
thized with them, lifted their sin-burden and made life more
hopeful for them. For this they crucified Him. And we shake
our heads and say: That just does not make sense!

At the present moment the world likewise is a world of dis-
sensions. Hatred, sabotage, distrust, deception sets man against
man, nation against nation. In homes, in business, in shops, in
political arenas, in church circles, in fact, everywhere people
are "scared to death" of one another. What shall we say?

Into this seething unrest of our times Christianity sets the
cross of Jesus and says: In Him you find the solution for all
the ills of life—*and peace.* As we do, the multitudes, who were
at each others throat, unite in a strange, determined fanati-
cism to oppose this Jesus and do away with His Gospel.

And why? What has He done? He has revealed the most
amazing love—while we were yet sinners He died for us. That
is what He has done: Died for us. And once more we shake
our heads and say: It does not make sense!

These *enemies* of the cross are found everywhere; not only
in atheistic countries and the seats of unbelieving scoffers.
Some of us have been, perchance, and are even now, *enemies
of the cross.* Let us see!

I. THE LEADERS OF JERUSALEM

The rulers, the spiritual leaders of Jerusalem, were enemies
of the cross. The high priest and the chief priests, the scribes,
and elders formed the deadly and the direct opposition to
Jesus, the Christ. These, forming the Sanhedrin of Jerusalem,
were to lead and guide the city in all spiritual truth, uphold
the Law and the prophets, and preserve in the conscience of
the people a sense of moral uprightness. Jesus was doing this
very thing as He moved about among them as the Prophet of
Galilee. "Think not that I am come to destroy the Law, or

the prophets: I am not come to destroy but to fulfill" (Matthew 5:17). Jesus gave the most idealistic interpretation of the Law. "Ye have heard that is was said by them of old time, Thou shalt not kill, and whosoever shall kill shall be in danger of the judgment: But I say unto you, that whosoever is angry with his brother without cause shall be in danger of judgment" (Matthew 5:21, 22). All who heard Jesus preach and teach bore witness to the graciousness of His words, for He did not speak as a scribe but as one having authority.

Yet the leaders of Jerusalem formed the most determined opposition. They mocked, they ridiculed, they jeered, spit into His face and demanded that He be crucified. Then—as Jesus hangs between heaven and earth, claimed neither by God nor man, they throw new gibes into His face. "He saved others, Himself He cannot save! Come down from the cross, if Thou be the Son of God! He trusted in God, let Him deliver Him now!" They admit that He trusted God and did many goodly deeds, yet they will not have Him. Why? Tell me, Why? Jesus disappointed them. He did "not play ball with them." He was weaning the people away from them. So Jesus did not fit into their scheme of things.

This is true to this day. With pet ideas and ideologies and man-made philosophies men set aside the Word and divide the church. They disagree among themselves and fight one another, yet they unite in their opposition to Christ Crucified. They will go along with the claim that Jesus is a great Reformer, a most remarkable man, but they revolt against being washed in the blood of the Lamb. They will have none of this. They even admit some people, the more gullible, get some peace and satisfaction out of this "blood religion" but with the same breath declare: We are beyond this "childish myth." Such are *enemies* of the cross, even though they parade as spiritual leaders of the day and in the church.

II. THE INDIFFERENT

Enemies of the cross are also they who pass by and are indifferent to the claims of Calvary. This type has no grievance, no peeves against the church; no ax to grind. They go with the crowd and do what the majority does and ask no questions and do no thinking. Enquire of them why they do this or believe that and they do not know. All they know is this, that around them people believe the same thing and follow the same standards.

A modern artist, Jean Beraud, has given us a take-off of the crucifixion in modern setting. All the characters on the way to Calvary are dressed in twentieth century clothing. In this painting I want to point out just one person: A boy about twelve. He stands in the foreground and attracts our attention the moment we look at the picture. He does not seem to know Jesus from Adam. He has been brought up modern. The mob rushes Jesus to Calvary where He is to be crucified. The boy runs along. He hears the jeering and sees some throwing stones. So he picks up one, too, and throws it at Jesus. And we ask why? Jesus never harmed him. In fact, the Jesus influence has given him a better world in which to live. Why then throw the stone? Just because the others are doing so. That is mob psychology. That makes him an enemy of the cross.

And are not we at times just as guilty! We are indifferent to the gospel, have no interest in Jesus, say all kinds of things about the childishness of being religious—all because someone has "wise-cracked" to an audience and everybody laughed and roared. So we think it smart to go with the crowd and talk disparagingly about the church and the Savior who gave His life for us. When we do—and do we not at times?—then we are aligning ourselves with that crowd which shouts: "Away with Him!"

III. CALLOUSED AND WORLDLY WISE

We come upon the third group at the foot of the cross: The soldiers who nailed Jesus' body to the tree. They are the calloused who have other interests. We find them thinking only

in materialistic terms. Garments are parceled out and change
is to be counted and divided between them. They know no
better way of getting what they want than by gambling at the
foot of the cross. They have no interest in Him whom they
have nailed to the beams. What change they can get out of the
chore is more important to them. The other interest is drink,
hard drinking to forget the boredom of life. In their loveless
carousals they see the suffering Savior and offer Him some of
their wine. They drink to the health of the Crucified. They
laugh and make their sport at the expense of a tortured soul.
Cold and callous they enjoy life which has no meaning nor
purpose to them. In fact, life is dirt cheap.

These soldiers have a counterpart in modern life. Religion
and the church may be alright for children, old people, and
"sissies." The church might be convenient to have in the community so that you may get a lift when you are down and out
or need a preacher for a funeral. But for the he-man and the
popular woman with charm the church is too tame. Appetite
is god. Enjoyment is the first order of the day. Such, drink to
the health of religion, it is true. They give their sop to the
Red Cross and the Community Chest and other welfare agen-
cies. That is the decent thing to do in order that you may have
some rating in the community and can make a polite tax re-
duction. But otherwise these say with the Gadarenes of Jesus'
day: "Let us alone! Do not bother us!"

IV. GRIEVANCES THAT KEEP US AWAY

We come still closer to that central cross on Calvary and
see a thief crucified with Jesus. He thinks he has a real
grievance and complaint to register against Jesus. Jesus has
not done a thing for him. Somehow this one thief knew that
Jesus had helped people out of their trouble. If he had lived
in Palestine, he could not have failed to know this Prophet of
Galilee had healed the sick and opened the eyes of the blind
and cleansed lepers. "Save Thyself and us," he exclaims. Never
in his life had he given up a thing for this Jesus, but now he

is in trouble and Jesus ought to get him out of his dilemma. So he thinks and so he says.

In place of being sympathetic, he is rebellious. He has been slighted. He is not given the consideration that he thinks he should have in his trouble and distress. He is being by-passed, neglected. "Save Thyself and us! Then I will believe."

In the modern church we have such people, too. Often they are you and I. We have not been made over. Our services have not been recognized. We were not praised as others. We think that others are pushed ahead at our expense. They get the office and we the work. They are appointed to important committees. We work just as hard but at no time is there any recognition from the leaders. So we become critical. We join the faultfinding club of the church. We are resentful and go through the day with a chip on our shoulder. With this behavior we join the ranks of the *enemies* of the cross.

V. THE ABSENTEES

Once more we look at the mob on Calvary's hill. We miss some that we expect to find there. In vain we look for the Twelve. Where are they? Where is Peter who so loudly and long had boasted in the Upper Room: "Lord, I am ready to go with Thee, both into prison, and to death" (Luke 22:33). The disciples had fled. Only one dared to come back and stand beneath the cross and say: "I belong!" In that crowd were undoubtedly some men and women whom Jesus had healed. There were fathers and mothers whose children Jesus had blessed. But you would never know it. They have hidden their identity; they are disciples in secret. They have not the courage to step forward and say: "He is our Friend!"

Such are colorless and valueless. They make no contribution to the cause of Christ and are no credit to the church. Like the chameleon they change color with every different association. We have quite a few of these in our twentieth century Christianity. Well might we ask: "Lord, is it I?" And the sad part of the story is this that we do not think ourselves *enemies* of the cross. We claim to be shrewd and wise and tactful. We boast that we know when to keep our mouth shut to stay out of trouble. Such are no help to the church and do themselves the greatest harm. Do they realize what comfort they give to the enemy? In war, as we all know, every solace given to the enemy by word or action is treason. Jesus likewise says: "He that is not with Me is against Me" (Luke 11: 23). Milling about in the enemies' camps, to hide out, makes us *enemies of the cross.*

As we look, then, a little closer into the faces of those on Calvary, that many-colored crowd of frenzied people, are we not compelled to say in terrified horror: "Why, he looks like me! It can't be; is it I?" Yet it is. So there is no time at the present for pointing fingers at others. Rather we should fall to our knees and say: "God be merciful to me!"

However, we dare not conclude without noting this fact that Jesus is right there in the center of Calvary. There where opposition, hatred, lovelessness, cowardliness, cruelty, brutality, and all that is mean and spiteful is seen in all its ugliness in man, there is lifted to the cross Jesus as Savior of the world. "Come down!" and Jesus refuses to do so. He stays there to die—that you and I might be forgiven. We *all*, in the church and out of the church, saved and unsaved, foremost citizens of the community and unknown slum dwellers, American-born or foreigners, *all* have sinned against this *greatheart* of love. Do we hear His plaintive cry at the Sea of Galilee: "Will ye also go away?" (John 6:67).

Today Jesus wants you and me to know that *the cross still stands.* There He hangs in the sight of all mankind with outstretched hands and bleeding heart, pleading and pleading and pleading: "Come to Me!" "And him that cometh, He will in no wise cast out."

6

THE PRAYERS OF THE CROSS

*"Father, forgive them; for they know
not what they do."*—Luke 23:34.
*"My God, My God, why hast Thou
forsaken Me?"*—Matthew 27:46.
*"Father, into Thy hands I commend
My Spirit."*—Luke 23:46.

Three times Jesus prayed on Calvary. The first prayer was made when He was nailed to the cross: "Father, forgive them; for they know not what they do." The second came out of that great darkness at midday: "Eli, Eli, lama sabachthani?" As Jesus bows His head in death, He prays once more to His Father, saying: "Father, into Thy hands I commend My spirit."

These prayers are more than an expression of a beautiful sentiment, more than the prayers of a martyr who has suffered great anguish and pain and is now going home to glory. These are the prayers of the suffering Servant, the Son of God made flesh, who took upon Himself the iniquity of us all. These prayers have a unique, saving value and reveal the Savior's great struggle with the forces of evil and His final victory over sin, death, and the powers of hell.

I. FATHER, FORGIVE THEM

This first prayer unmasks to us the deadliness of sin. Sin can so paralyze the conscience that sin no longer appears as sin. Even the devil seeks to disguise himself as an angel of light (cf. 2 Corinthians 11:14). Therefore Jesus prays: "Forgive them, for they know not what they do." Did the soldiers not know that they were nailing this Jesus to the cross and

causing Him untold pain? Driving those nails through hands
and feet would cause many to faint. These soldiers were aware
of this and therefore had brought along sour wine which could
be given to ease the pain.

However, they did not realize that God was being nailed to
the cross. They thought that this Jesus was just another criminal, who had done something deserving of death by crucifixion according to Roman Law. In this sense they did not know
what they were doing; neither did many who looked on, and
then mocked and jeered at Jesus and joined the leaders in
throwing insults and abuse at their Savior.

Methinks, that we too must admit that time and again our
sins do not register with us. We do these sins in our waking
hour but are not awake to their sinfulness. We lie, and we
know it, but dismiss lies with a shrug of the shoulder and call
it a "fib," which does not amount to much. We say unkind
words, but excuse them by saying that these people had to be
told off and put in their place. We do not attend divine
services, too busy with our routine work, and say: We have to
eat, or, We can always go to church some other time. So we
make light of sin and do not realize that each and every transgression of the will of God grieves the Lord and separates us
from Him. Sin, no matter how tiny it seems to us, *is* SIN in the
sight of God, spelled with capital letters.

Jesus prays: "Father, *forgive*." No matter how trivial sin
appears to us, it *must* be removed, if we are to stand in the
presence of the holy God. Ignorance does not excuse us. That
is why David prays: "Cleanse Thou me from secret faults"
(Psalm 19:12).

All—Through Christ

These sins must be blotted out, cancelled, taken away, forgiven. This can be done only through Christ's blood, shed on
Calvary. He must blot out *all* sin; not merely the heinous, the
brutal, the vicious, the scandalous sins; not only those which
public opinion condemns and frowns upon; not merely those

for which the government sends trangressors to prison; not
merely those which the church brands as unbecoming a
Christian: *All* sin—those which God and *we* only know; sins
which even society approves and which are considered natural
failings, a part of our personality. Yes, all sin, each and every
sin against God, against our fellowmen, even against ourselves, in thought, in word, in conduct, known or unknown,
must be forgiven if we are to stand in the presence of God.
And every sin must be forgiven and cancelled *through Christ*
who hangs on that accursed tree. God is holy; God is just. God
cannot wink at sin. Some one must pay for every sin committed. Only Jesus can and Jesus does. That is why He prays:
Father, forgive, for I am suffering for them; I am atoning and
making good for their transgressions. Even if we are not aware
of this fact and do not understand all our secret sins, they
must be paid for with blood and life. This is God's decree.
This you and I must know. For this reason, each one must
single out himself and learn how deadly sin is to our own soul.
Jesus is pleading *for me*. Jesus also prayed *for me* on Calvary:
"Father, forgive." Only if we realize this to be the fact and
eternal truth can we find forgiveness, peace, and healing from
each and every sin.

II. "MY GOD, MY GOD"

The second prayer lets us look into the depths of the judgments of God over sin and see at what tremendous price we
were delivered from the clutches of Satan, as Jesus pleads:
"My God, My God, why hast Thou forsaken Me?"

This prayer gives voice to a soul in utmost distress. Forsaken
of God! The Son is separated from His Father because of
man's sin. Forsaken! This is not an earthly experience. No
one, not even the criminal, is utterly forsaken of God in this
present world. As long as we breathe, eat, sleep, even in a
coma and out of mind, we are not altogether and completely
forsaken of God.

God drove Adam out of the garden, but before Adam left

Eden to toil in the sweat of his brow, God promised him and the human race the Messiah who would crush the serpent's head and break the power of the devil. This pledge to Adam gives also to you and me a hope in a world filled with sorrow and tears and assures us a peaceful departure as we stand at the portals of eternity.

Cain became a fugitive and vagabond on earth, restless and guilt-conscious; yet God set a mark on him that none, seeing him, could kill him. Judas betrayed his Savior and Friend and lost and was lost. However, even Judas cannot say that Jesus did not want him. Even at the very moment of the betrayal in Gethsemane, Jesus said to him: "Friend, wherefore art thou come?" "Judas, betrayest thou the Son of man with a kiss?" (Matthew 26:50; Luke 22:48) .

Even the wicked are not totally forsaken, for God gives even to them sunshine and rain, the air they breathe, and the life they have. The ungodly prosper and enjoy their food, and sometimes the righteous and Christian complain to God that He is too good to such as ignore Him and His Gospel and offend Him with their sins. Yet God patiently takes care of their needs; perchance they may come to realize the goodness of God and be led to the cross and be saved.

There is a Hell

Only one place is to be found, where one is forsaken altogether: in hell. That is where Jesus went as He was wrapped in that significant darkness of Calvary. In that forsakenness Jesus paid the penalty of sin in full for the whole world. However, in hell He held fast to His God and prayed: *My God.* "Forsaken!" but wonder of wonders, Jesus does not despair. He prays. That word "MY" gave power to this prayer and atoned and made good for the sins of all sinners. The ransom price which releases us who have transgressed the Law of God is paid and our salvation is finished and complete.

There is a hell. Scripture teaches this. And Jesus, more than any other, has spoken about this abode of the lost, who are forever forsaken of God. This hell is not an earthly experience, though some may have a foretaste of it in this present life. Life may be full of heartaches, suffering, wickedness, and sorrow, but this is not hell. Jesus went with our sin into that hell of eternity, the abode of the devil, to crush the serpent's head, and to release the grip of Satan on the souls of humanity and set us free.

Jesus is forsaken because of *our* sins. Sin has darkened man's thinking, turned our desires into lusts, and our conduct into lawlessness. Man lives in rebellion against God by nature, as Romans 1 so graphically depicts. Man is in constant conflict with his fellowmen, selfish, greedy, grasping. *We* go astray, *we* err, *we* defy God, and are inhuman in our brutality. All this causes Jesus to be forsaken of God, because on *Him* was laid *our* sin. He is serving sentence *for us.* Jesus, the Crucified, *died for me* and was *forsaken* that *we* need not be forsaken of God in time nor in eternity.

This is the heart of Christianity's Gospel. Remove this historic fact from Calvary and this truth from the Gospel, that Jesus was forsaken for us, and there is no Gospel. Then each and everyone must make good for his own sins. Our only claim on heaven is found in this truth and fact that Jesus *was* forsaken and still clung to His Father and prays: *My God!*

In these hours of darkness the greatest battle of history was fought and the victory of the ages and time was won. So gruelling and so gruesome was this life-and-death battle that God covered the earth with darkness that none with human eyes should see. However, we know and must know the outcome. We do. The Son of God on that cross cried with a loud voice: "It is finished!"

III. "FATHER, INTO THY HANDS"

This brings us to the third prayer of the cross: "Father, into Thy hands I commend My spirit." This prayer reveals the peace which that heart has found. The mind is at ease as the soul is done with sin. A complete reconciliation has been consummated. A mutual undertanding is effected. Jesus has finished the work and satisfactorily performed the task for which He became flesh and dwelled among the children of men. The sacrifice and the ransom-price have met every requirement of the Law. Everything is paid in full.

Jesus has done all this for you and me. We now are reconciled. We need not worry about sin, as long as we stand beneath the cross. There is no condemnation for us who are in Christ Jesus. We live in grace. Death has no sting. With Simon, we believers can say: "Lord, now lettest Thou Thy servant depart in peace." We can and should make Jesus' prayer *our* prayer in the dying hours of our life: "Father, into Thy hands I commend my spirit." Death becomes a sleep and a going home, made possible through Christ's death and resurrection. Judgment to come holds no terror. "Being justified by faith, we have peace with God through our Lord Jesus Christ" (Romans 5:1). In the courts of God we shall be acquitted because we are clothed in the garments of Christ's holiness. Jesus is our Advocate and Lawyer, who pleads our case as our perfect Savior.

Perfect Bliss Through Christ

For us eternity holds perfect bliss, which fullness of joy awaits us in the presence of God forevermore. There we shall be like the risen Lord. Our dust-body, raised on that last day, shall stand in His presence to praise Him as the Lamb upon the throne and that with saints and angels. There God shall wipe away all tears from our eyes and suffering shall be unknown. This aching self, frought with handicaps and shortcomings, shall be perfect, as the first Adam in the beginning of time. There all heartaches shall be removed and all misunderstandings be cleared up. Love shall be supreme in the presence of God, who is Love.

There, all mysteries shall be solved. In this world we are daily confronted with the questions of Why and Wherefore. But around God's throne there is no darkness and there are no mysteries. There we shall understand and praise God who moved in His own mysterious ways to perform the wonders of our ultimate salvation.

All this is eternal, permanent. In this world we reach the height of joy at one moment and the next we are sad unto death. But in that eternity of heaven there shall be fullness of joy and pleasure forevermore. All this is because on Calvary Jesus suffered and died and shed His blood that heaven might be *our* home. To His disciples in the Upper Room Jesus said: "In My Father's house are many mansions: if it were not so, I would have told you. I go to prepare a place for you. And if I go and prepare a place for you, I will come again, and receive you unto Myself, that where I am, there ye may be also" (John 14:2, 3).

As Jesus, then, prays His last prayer before He bows His head in death, "Father, into Thy hands I commend My spirit," He does so with that confidence that the task is done and mankind redeemed. And the guarantee to this eternal truth? Jesus' resurrection only a few hours away. This gives us the assurance that He who lives has made for us a life eternal in the glories of heaven.

Let us thank God for these three prayers of the cross. As we hear these prayers, let us rejoice and praise God who sent His Son, made flesh, to crush Satan and sin and make our death a homegoing to His very throne. The cost of our redemption was tremendous, but it has made sure our salvation. Nothing has been left undone. We cannot add a whit. In Jesus and His cross which still stands is peace and hope and heaven. How can we ever again be indifferent to His plea: "Come and find rest for your souls!"

> Were the whole realm of nature mine
> That were a tribute far too small;
> Love so amazing, so divine,
> Demands my soul, my life, *my all.*

7

THE COMPANIONS OF THE CROSS

*"Now there stood by the cross of Jesus His mother,
and His mother's sister, Mary the wife of Cleophas,
and Mary Magdalene. When Jesus therefore saw
His mother, and the disciple standing by, whom
He loved, He saith unto His mother, Woman, behold
thy son! Then saith He to the disciple, Behold thy
mother! And from that hour that disciple took her
unto his own home."—*John 19:25-27.

Loyalty is at a premium at all times. With what satisfaction
we read the story of David and Jonathan! "The soul of Jonathan was knit with the soul of David, and Jonathan loved him
as his own soul" (1 Samuel 18:1). Because of his devotion
to David, Jonathan faced the anger and displeasure of his
own father, king Saul. The king at one time threw a javelin
in a fit of anger at his own son because Jonathan with courage
and unabated loyalty defended his friend David. How we
rejoice to know that David never forgot the value of this
friendship! As David came to the throne and enjoyed the
advantages of the kingdom, he remembered Jonathan, long
dead, and asked if any of Jonathan's children still were alive.
David was told of Mephibosheth, a son of Jonathan, a cripple,
who was hiding away in fear of his life. Remembering Jonathan, David had Mephibosheth brought to the palace to eat
at the king's table till the end of his life. (cf. 2 Samuel 9).

Jesus likewise stresses the importance of faithfulness. "Be
thou faithful unto death!" is His admonition. "He that shall
endure to the end, the same shall be saved," is His promise.
Jesus never turned from any who came to Him with the

burdens of life. With understanding compassion He lifted them to His heart of love.

We are not surprised, are we, to find loyal and faithful companions beneath the cross? No matter what one has done in life, some one among friends will stand by us. Jesus has done so much to lift humanity out of its misery. We are rather dumbfounded that so few rally to His side. Where is Simon Peter, who boasted that he would rather die than deny his Lord! Where is Matthew who had forsaken the tax collector's table to follow Jesus! Where is James—and Andrew? Where are those whom Jesus cleansed from the loathed leprosy? Where are those whose eyes were opened that they may see, and where are the lame and the halt?

But why ask about these, when we ourselves are often so indifferent, making flimsy excuses and finding endless number of alibis for failing to say: I belong. Must not Jesus confront us, too, with the plaintive question: "What! could ye not watch with Me one hour?" Are we at our accustomed place to worship the Savior who gave His life for us? Our loyalties lag, too. Four out of the thousands who knew Jesus stood beneath the cross, loyal and faithful. They arrest our attention. While the wild-eyed mob jeers and defiantly demands that He come down from the cross, these four dared to stand there and say: We still love Him and will stand by Him and with Him to the end. *Who are they?*

I. MARY, THE WIFE OF CLEOPHAS

By the cross of Jesus stood Mary, the wife of Cleophas, a sister of the mother of Jesus. This is the only time that she is called the "wife of Cleophas." She is the mother of James and Jude, two of the disciples of Jesus. She is definitely designated as the sister of the mother of Jesus. To us it seems strange that the two sisters should have the same name and the Bible does not tell us why. Some think that this Mary was much older and had left the household when the younger sister was born. Some also think that she is the wife of that

Cleophas who went to Emmaus on the first Easter afternoon and that this Mary was his partner. However, this is doubtful and of no consequence to us. This Mary came with her sister, the mother of Jesus, and her nephew John to Calvary and stood at the cross. She is genuinely concerned about this Jesus, her nephew. She is solicitous about her sister's well-being. While some of Jesus' relatives had said: "He is beside Himself!" she was sympathetic and loyal to the cause of Jesus. She believed Him to be the Messiah, promised of old.

She came *and stood*. That is all that is said of her. But the fact is eternally true: *She stood there*. She identifies herself with the cause of Jesus, whom all Jerusalem rejected and demanded to be crucified. Standing there, she stood at the right place. She stood where we all should stand, always, beneath the cross. This was not an easy thing to do, as the frenzied mob was milling to and fro, liable to attack any one who favored the condemned Prophet. It was not a popular thing to do at this moment; rather, it was dangerous.

Where Do We Stand

What brought this Mary to Calvary? Her deep and abiding love for Jesus. This alone will bring forth a full confession from the lips of any of us. To do so we *must* have the conviction that He alone saves. The Law condemns. Our own accomplishments fall short. Our possessions cannot pay the price of redemption. Only Jesus could, because He was the Son of God. If we believe this, then we will say:"Lord, to whom shall we go? Thou hast the words of eternal life. And we believe and are sure that Thou art that Christ, the Son of the living God" (John 6:68, 69).

This Mary stands for that large group of unnoticed believers, who serve Jesus unheralded and unsung. You can count on them, as a rule, to be at their place as we worship, as we commune, as we are called upon to show our hands. Often such get no pat on the shoulder, receive no praise. They stand in the shadows rather than in the limelight. But they live quietly their Christian lives and no one can be mistaken about their faith and their allegiance. They never question the Lordship of their Savior. To live such unrecognized and unheralded lives takes a lot of Christian grace. Yet these are so important to the lifeline of the church, these rank-and-file people. Everybody knows that they belong and what they are. This is the loyalty which you and I must show. We must stand at the cross and let all the world know that we are Christians.

II. MARY FROM MAGDALA

By that cross stood Mary Magdalene. She was not related to the family of Jesus. She came from Magdala, a small village on the northern shores of the Sea of Galilee. She had been demon-possessed, for Jesus had driven seven devils out of her. By this miracle of grace Jesus had brought two things into her life. She had found *peace* of heart and mind. Those terrible inner conflicts were gone. Her mind was at ease as she made sure of the divine forgiveness so graciously given by Jesus. Her life no longer was in the grip of Satan.

She also found *purpose* to her life. That restless, aimless vacuum had gone out of her day. She had something worthwhile to do. With other women she served Jesus with her earthly possessions. Jesus and His disciples depended upon her and other women for financial aid. Appreciative of all that Jesus had done for her, she stood beneath that cross and came early on that Easter morn to the tomb with the other women, to see if anything more could be done. She would not fail her Savior even in His deepest humiliation.

The Christ-Filled Life

And what are *we* to learn from this example of devotion and loyalty? Is it not this that after all the Christ-filled life is indeed a most satisfying life? The Christian has treasures which rust and thieves cannot take from him. In the loneliest hours of the journey we Christians are not alone. We have a Friend whose abiding presence spells peace and gives us the grace to adjust ourselves to situations which for the time being cannot be changed. In the hour of death we have Him who leads us through—not around in—but through the valley of death to the glory of His throne in heaven.

We see then in Mary Magdalene the gratitude of a redeemed soul. This thankful heart expresses itself in a service unstintingly and joyously given. The Christian places all at the feet of the Savior and knows the joy and the blessedness of giving and sharing. This loyalty did not remain unrecognized. Jesus, too, is appreciative. Mary Magdalene was the first to see the *risen Lord* and the *first* to tell the disciples the great Easter message: The Lord is risen! Jesus lives!

As we ponder on these things are we not compelled to ask ourselves: Just how rich has my life been in Christ and for Christ? Can we say with Paul: "I have fought the good fight. I have kept the faith?" (2 Timothy 4:7).

III. MARY, THE MOTHER OF JESUS

At the cross stood Mary, the mother of Jesus. You would expect her to be there. Even if Jesus had been guilty of the most unspeakable crimes, Mary still would have been there. She knew, however, that in Him was no sin. Love, mother love, brought her there and kept her there till the end. As she stands there, she utters not a word. Silently she endures. Does she recall Simeon's words, spoken many years ago at the Temple: "A sword shall pierce through thy own soul also?" (Luke 2:35). Filled with faith and piety, she stands there uncomplainingly, knowing that God's will was being done for the salvation of many. Though she may not fully have understood the total significance of this death of her Son, nevertheless she was sure that He was doing that for which He came into the world: Save all humanity from the clutches of sin and give mankind a new hope.

We see no hysterical Mary, crying out against "man's inhumanity to man." There is no rebellious demonstration against the ways of God. She knows that God's thoughts are higher than ours and that this her Son as "That Holy Thing" must die that God's good and gracious will be done and fulfilled in us. Her love for her human Son did not embitter her heart against the divine plan of redemption because she must suffer this anguish of heart.

No Immunity from Trouble

Thousands of faithful Christians have faced crosses which seemed impossible to bear. With anguished heart they have exclaimed: "Why has this befallen me?" Yet with Mary they have said: "Thy will be done," and felt sure that God's will is always gracious. Though we do not understand we believe that we cannot perish, because God gave His Son to redeem us from the judgments of sin and death to give us life eternal. God has not promised us Christians immunity from the troubles of life, but He has promised us the crown of life after we enter the portals of eternity. As we face such ordeals as Mary did at the cross, seeing her Son die amid the mockery of the multitude, God will give us, at all times, the needed strength to stand up under the burden. Even though we look through a glass darkly and do not know why our burden should be especially so heavy, in eternity we shall yet praise God for the way of sorrow which has led us to that glory where God shall wipe away all tears from our eyes.

Even if a mother's love should turn against her child, yet God's love in Christ never ceases to flow toward you and me, daily and richly. His love will never let go. Such is God's promise: "Can a woman forget her sucking child, that she should not have compassion on the son of her womb? yea, they may forget, yet will I not forget thee. Behold, I have graven thee upon the palms of My hands" (Isaiah 49:15, 16). Therefore, God and our Savior expect us to stand with Mary, His mother, beneath the cross, where He brings healing in His wings.

IV. JOHN, THE BELOVED DISCIPLE

At that cross stood John, the faithful disciple and friend of

Jesus. He too stands there in loyal devotion. He alone of all the disciples dares to come. As he stands there, Jesus places upon him a responsibility and obligation: To take His mother under his protection and care. John was especially suitable for this task. He was one of Jesus' closest friends and also a relative. And he was young. This request demanded service and sacrifice. As the days would go on, Mary would grow older and feeble and become a heavier responsibility. But John accepts the directive and life becomes richer and fuller as the years go on. He is faithful to his Friend. That is why he was there. He was eager to render this attention to Mary out of loyalty to Jesus, taking her to his home and caring for her until her death. The task was well done, because he loved his Savior.

What about us? Can we face the Savior of the world and say: We have done our best with the abilities and the wherewiths which we possess. One thing Jesus requires of us, looks for in us, both young and old, that we be found faithful. Jesus expects us to stand in our place of duty and to assume our responsibilities and to meet all our obligations with dutiful regularity. The widow in Jesus' day gave less than any other that day when Jesus stood at the treasury in the Temple courts. By the standards of man the amount was not worth mentioning. You could not even buy a sparrow with those two mites. However, according to Jesus' evaluation of things those two coins amounted to more than all the moneys the others had placed into the treasuries. Jesus asks that we serve Him with all our heart and all our strength. We should do the best with what we have and that in appreciation of His Calvary sacrifice.

John's Important Testimony

Another thing is to be said of John: He bears witness with conviction to the greatest and most important fact in history: Jesus was pierced, and *shed* His blood. "But one of the soldiers with a spear pierced His side, and forthwith came there out blood and water. And he that saw it bare record, and his record is true; and he knoweth that he saith true, that ye might believe" (John 19:34, 35). John was eyewitness to this historic fact, proclaimed in prophecy as a mark of the Messiah, that Jesus as the Lamb of God gave His life *by the shedding of blood*. Life is in the blood and that sacrifice in blood must be made for sin. Our Christian religion is not a cheap religion. It cost the life-blood of the Son of God, made flesh. This John wants you and me to know. Of this we are to be sure. Under fire John confessed to this truth. And why? That you and I, living centuries later, might be certain that this Jesus as foretold by prophecy *shed* His blood on Calvary and therefore *is* the Messiah. If so, then we are saved and at peace with God, for atonement has been made in full for all our sin.

Another fact should be stressed: John would not budge an inch in making this assertion. He insisted that he witnessed this *shedding* of blood. He would not compromise this historic fact, for this is the life-and-death truth of our Christian faith. With this fact Christianity stands and falls, for "without shedding of blood is no remission of sin" (Hebrews 9:22). This points a question at you and me: Have we such convictions? Do we uncompromisingly accept that Jesus *shed* His blood that we might be forgiven? Are we ready to take to consequences in defending this truth and fact of Calvary over and against the enemies and compromisers of the cross? Or are we looking for a "soft" Christianity which stands for nothing and contributes nothing to the Gospel of the cross? Jesus Himself tells us: "He that is not with Me is against Me" (Luke 11:23).

You and I have enjoyed the friendship of Jesus over the years. He has chosen us. Therefore we stand in His grace, where we enjoy the treasures which are eternal: Forgiveness, peace, hope, heaven. How loyal are we to Him, who gave His life and shed His blood for our redemption? John saw his Friend shed His blood. He saw in this Friend more than a friend. He saw in Jesus his Savior. Sin was *on* Jesus, yet *in* Jesus was no sin. Now John knew that all his own sins were blotted out, "for the blood of Jesus Christ His Son cleanseth us from all sin" (1 John 1:7).

You and I also have a sin-problem, a serious one. Surely we are not deceiving ourselves into believing and saying that we have never sinned or that sin does not amount to much! Only under the cross shall we realize how greatly we have sinned and find the solution and cure and healing from sin. At the cross we find peace with God, and only there. And do not let anyone tell you anything different!

8

THE VICTORY OF THE CROSS

*"When Jesus therefore had received
the vinegar, He said, It is finished."*
—John 19:30.

In the Greek we have only one word, announcing the victory of the cross: *Tetelestai—done.* Ever since, the sinner has a hope that never fades nor fails and a salvation that is sure and certain.

Done—finished. "He was wounded for our transgressions"—but no more. He was crucified and died—but no more. He was buried—but no more. He lives as victorious Savior. Salvation is a completed fact, with nothing left undone. And this salvation is for you and me. *Done*—and now even almighty God cannot condemn you and me as we stand beneath the cross, cleansed by and through the blood of His own Son. This *is* gospel, the best newscast ever told to mankind.

I. THE SUFFERING FINISHED

Done—finished is the *suffering* of Him who took upon Himself the sin of the world. Although in Jesus was no sin, and therefore He ought not to have suffered any pain, much less tasted death, yet He endured greater pain and went through the agony of the damned, because He was substituting for the whole race of man. That is why we hear Him exclaiming in the darkness of those three hours: "My God, My God, why hast Thou forsaken Me?" But now it is done, the agony of the cross. This is more than a cry of relief, announcing that the torture is over after six hours on Calvary. Some time we thank God that death has come. We have seen a child or a friend suffering for weeks, maybe months, in a lingering illness and we are grateful that death has brought life to a close. However, this cry is more than a cry of relief.

This was the shout of victory, announcing to three worlds that Jesus had won. Heaven is told and the angels rejoice; hell learns of the victory and trembles; the peoples of the earth hear the good news and know that the guilt and blame and the curse of sin is taken away. We can look up without trembling and say to the angel of death: Take me home to my Savior, for I am redeemed and saved. Jesus has proclaimed His victory over sin, death, and the devil with this glorious manifesto: *It is finished!*

Jesus did on that cross what the saintliest of men could not do for self—save his own soul. Man has tried—but found no peace in his accomplishments. The Aztec Indians chose annually the finest of their young men and placed him on the sacrificial altar and cut open his breast and tore out his heart to appease the gods. The Flagellantes of Europe would beat themselves with their flagellum till they fell exhausted to the ground from the loss of blood. The Dervishes of the Mohammedan ascetic orders dance their exotic dances until they fall fainting to the ground. All this is done to free the soul from the guilt of sin and the accusing conscience. But in the end the cry rises from the distressed heart: Is this enough?

Salvation a Finished Fact

Jesus also suffered untold agony, but, as the eternal God made flesh. This is why He became human that He might suffer and die for the sins that we humans have committed. When He cried out with a loud voice: "It is finished," He was announcing to man, angels, and devils that He had accomplished the salvation of man, that He had atoned for the sins of the whole world with His life-blood. This proclamation of the completed redemption Jesus "backed up" with His resurrection on the third day. Then the tomb was empty and He was seen alive. Mary Magdalene, the other women,

Simon Peter, the Emmaus disciples, the Twelve behind
closed doors, saw the risen Lord. Salvation was a finished fact.

The Greatest Feat in History

By finishing this salvation of man, Jesus accomplished
the greatest feat in history. No greater or more decisive battle
was ever fought than that of Calvary. Ambitious man has
undertaken great things through the centuries and succeeded
in science, in medicine, in new discoveries on earth and in
space and under the sea. But no man has ever been able to
make atonement for sins which he has committed. Eagerly
man has undertaken adventurous programs and accomplishing the seemingly impossible. Men have been filled with the
lust for power and made war to get all for self no matter how
many had to die. Others have sought to make the world
safe for democracy and still are trying. Oh! the failures and
the disappointments of life! None ever saved the human race
from sin!

Jesus undertook the greatest task in history, saving the
human race from the damnation of hell. This He accomplished. Even though He bowed His head in death and was
in the tomb till the third day, Jesus knew that He had won
the greatest victory. Therefore He shouted with a loud voice:
"It is finished!"

And what does this mean to you and me? My guilt problem is solved, for my sin is removed and the penalty of my
guilt paid in full by Jesus the Crucified. Therefore my salvation is an accomplished fact. I cannot add one iota or one
mill or cent to this perfect sacrifice that my perfect Savior
made for me. That is the message of the victory cry: I am,
with Christ, sharing the conquest over sin and death and hell.
The demands of the Law of Sinai have been met and I am
free through faith in this Christ who gave His life that I might
live. The grip of sin is broken, death has lost its sting and has
become a sleep and a home-going. I can resist the temptations

of Satan and tell him: Get thee hence! Christ's victory is victory for me.

II. PROPHECY FULFILLED

Done—It is finished. Another fact is established through this cry: Jesus has fulfilled all prophecy concerning the Messiah and thereby has established for all time to come that He is the Christ, the Son of the living God. Throughout His life and His Passion we are told that Jesus did certain things that prophecy might be fulfilled. All of these are—so says Jesus: Finished! Three times in these dying moments Scripture relates that this was done to fulfill prophecy. Which are these?

"Jesus knowing that all things were now accomplished, that the Scripture might be fulfilled, saith, I thirst" (John 19:28). Did any prophecy of the Old Testament speak of this thirsting? We turn to Psalm 69:21 where we read: "They gave Me also gall for My meat; and in My thirst they gave Me vinegar to drink."

Then John records: "But when they came to Jesus, and saw that He was dead already, they brake not His legs . . . for these things were done, that Scripture should be fulfilled, A bone of Him shall not be broken." As we page back to Psalm 34:20 we read: "He keepeth all His bones; not one of them is broken." Jesus was the true Lamb of God and this fact, that a bone was not to be broken, had special significance. As Israel left Egypt that Passover night, God told them that ever after they should eat yearly the Passover lamb. In doing so, they were not to break a bone in the animal. Since Jesus *is* the Lamb of God which is taking away the sin of the world on Calvary's cross, not one bone of His body is to be broken. This was sign and evidence that He truly was the Messiah.

Only Jesus Pierced

Again John writes: "But one of the soldiers with a spear pierced His side. . . . And again another Scripture saith,

They shall look on Him whom they pierced." This is stated
in Zechariah 12:10. And David has the suffering Messiah
say in Psalm 22:16: "They pierced My hands and My feet."

As we ponder on this thirsting, the non-breaking of the
bones and the piercing of His hands and feet and side, we
are truly confronted by unusual incidents. Visualize to yourself this scene! Three men are hanging side by side on Calvary. Two of them have their legs broken, but Jesus is passed
by. Remember, the soldier who does not break the legs of
Jesus, knows nothing of this prophetic statement. On the
other hand, Jesus receives the spearthrust and "forthwith
came there out blood and water." The other two are *not*
pierced. It almost seems incredible that this should happen.
We see here definitely the finger of God the Father who
points to this Jesus and says: This is My Messiah, the official
Lamb which takes away the sin of the world.

Jesus is fully aware of all this. So He called out with a
loud voice: "It is finished!" The prophecies concerning the
Messiah are fulfilled in Me. I am He who came to seek and to
save the lost of the world. But more! If Jesus has fulfilled the
Messianic prophecies which had to do with His dwelling
among the children of men, then we can feel certain that
all the *other* foretellings of Him and by Him shall be fulfilled in due time.

Jesus has promised that His abiding presence shall pro-
tect His church until the end of days. No matter how gloomy
the outlook may appear to our dimmed eyes, His cause shall
triumph. The gates of hell shall not prevail. Even in this
New Testament dispensation Satan's power is limited. Christ's
presence protects His church and us. Satan cannot pluck us
out of His hands.

Once more, Jesus tells us that He shall come again in glory
to judge the living and the dead. The scoffer sneers: "Where
is the promise of His coming!" But the signs of His return are
being fulfilled before our very eyes as wars and rumors of
wars persist, as false prophets and false Christs arise, as the

gospel is being radioed to the uttermost parts of the world. As these prophecies are being "finished," we can be certain that Christ is coming in triumph to celebrate the Calvary victory with saints and angels throughout eternity.

III. THE OLD TESTAMENT CEREMONIES ARE FINISHED

Done—It is finished! The Old Testament sacrifices of lambs and bullocks and turtle doves is a thing of the past. So says the writer of the Hebrews: "For such a high priest became us, who is holy, harmless, undefiled, separate from sinners, and made higher than the heavens; Who needed not daily, as those high priests, to offer up sacrifice first for his own sins, and then for the people's; for this He did once, when He offered up Himself" (Hebrews 7:26; 27). "Now where remission of these [sins] is, there is no more offering for sin" (Hebrews 10:18). No more do we Christians of the New Testament age bring blood sacrifices. In the Old Testament these were a type, pointing to the coming Messiah. However, the Messiah-Christ is here. He made the *real* sacrifice on Calvary. Therewith the ceremonial laws of Moses are abolished. This Jesus wants all the world to know. Therefore He cried out with a loud voice: "Finished!"

We too are to tell the world that no more blood sacrifices are required, made by priests at the sacrificial altar. As prophets, as preachers, as witnesses for Christ we are to tell the world that all is done: Mankind *is* redeemed through the cross. This we do in a special manner as we come to the Lord's Table. We are to remember that we are the beneficiaries of this Calvary sacrifice, receiving the full assurance of a complete forgiveness of all sin, as He gives us with the bread and the cup His Body and Blood. Each time we come to the Upper Room with the awareness of sin and plead for mercy, we are washed, cleansed, healed, and restored to grace. We leave the Table with a faith strengthened to resist sin and Satan and go on with courage and confidence. We have the promise that our gracious Savior will go with us to journey's end. Christ did the sacrificing; we do the remembering and the receiving of forgiveness and faith. Each time we come to the Sacramental Altar, we can say with Simon of old: "Lord, now lettest Thou Thy servant depart in peace."

To know that Jesus Christ was the Victor of the cross, conquering sin, death, and hell, we too can live victorious lives. With Paul we can say: "I can do all things through Christ which strengtheneth me" (Philippians 4:13). The burden of guilt is lifted; sin is removed. The love of God watches over us. So we need not worry. We are safe and secure, for the cross underwrites heaven for us.

Done—It is finished! The victory is won. Because Jesus finished for us this salvation, we can come to the end of the road as pilgrims of the Way, saying with Paul: "I have fought a good fight; I have finished my course, I have kept the faith. Henceforth there is laid up for me a crown of righteousness, which the Lord, the righteous Judge, shall give me at that day" (2 Timothy 4:7, 8). "For I know whom I have believed, and am persuaded that He is able to keep that which I have committed unto Him against that day" (2 Timothy 1:12). And *what* have I committed to Him, my Savior? My soul which He has redeemed with His own blood on the cross of Calvary. This is certain and sure, for Jesus exclaimed with a loud voice: "It is finished!"

DONE!

9

THE CONFESSORS OF THE CROSS

> *"And as they led Him away, they laid hold upon one Simon, a Cyrenian, coming out of the country, and on him they laid the cross, that he might bear it after Jesus."*—Luke 23:26
>
> *"And he said unto Jesus, Lord, remember me when Thou comest into Thy kingdom. And Jesus said unto him, Verily, I say unto thee, Today shalt thou be with Me in Paradise."*—Luke 23:42, 43
>
> *"And when the centurion, which stood over and against Him, saw that He so cried out, and gave up the ghost, he said: Truly this was the Son of God."*—Mark 15:39
>
> *"And after this Joseph of Arimathea, being a disciple of Jesus, but secretly for fear of the Jews, besought Pilate that he might take away the body of Jesus: and Pilate gave him leave. He came therefore, and took the body of Jesus. And there came also Nicodemus, which at the first came to Jesus by night, and brought a mixture of myrrh and aloes, about an hundred pound weight. Then took they the body of Jesus, and wound it in linen clothes with spices, as the manner of the Jews is to bury"*
> —John 19:38-40.

Five men came forward on that crucifixion day of Jesus and identified themselves with Him. Theirs is an unusual story. Three of these were compelled to witness the crucifixion from the beginning to the end; the other two were latecomers on Calvary that day, arriving after the death of Jesus. Two, most likely, never had heard of this Jesus until this Passover Friday; one might have known that another was up in Galilee starting sedition against Rome; a fourth identified himself secretly with Jesus; and a fifth who had interviewed Jesus to learn a little more about Him kept himself aloof for expediency's sake. On that Good Friday all indentified themselves with Jesus.

I. SIMON OF CYRENE

The first to come into the limelight is Simon of Cyrene. He is standing on the sidelines as Jesus is led to Calvary, wondering what all this excitement meant. He was merely looking on. He was not one of the mob, jeering and shouting, and screaming: "Crucify Him!" He was an uninterested passerby. He just happened along and stepped aside to let the gruesome procession and the howling mob go on. However it was he whom the centurion picked out of the mass of people to carry the cross after Jesus. The condemned Jesus had fallen from exhaustion and loss of blood under the weight of the cross. The centurion realized that the Nazarene would be unable to reach Calvary under His own cross. The officer needed help. According to Roman Law he had the right to draft anyone into service which did not require him to go beyond the radius of two miles. The Roman's eyes fell on this Cyrenian, standing on the roadside and demanded that he come forward and carry the cross for the condemned man. He was compelled to follow orders, forced to render this service. Undoubtedly he resented doing this chore. He did not come to Jerusalem for this kind of task. No honor or distinction went with this service. Yet this duty, unwillingly performed, brought him to Calvary to witness the crucifixion of Jesus. At that cross he became a convert.

How do we know? Scripture tells us so. Simon had two sons, Alexander and Rufus, who are numbered among the Christians of the Jerusalem Church (cf. Mark 15:21). The carrying of the cross after Jesus was by the grace of God the making of Simon spiritually.

From this account of the life of Simon we might learn some valuable lessons. Often, like Simon, we resent certain happenings taking place in our church and community activities. Some task is assigned to us, some obligation laid upon us which is distasteful to us. For the time being we pout and become critical of every one and everything. However, in time we discover that these unpleasant assignments have been training schools for greater and better service. Through such incidents we are brought closer to Jesus. These were not of our making. Some misfortune, not brought on by ourselves, or some sin which others have done, placed on us double duties and extra burdens. Out of these situations come, however, a deeper appreciation of the Gospel, a new outlook of life, a development of character and a growth in Christian faith. Through these trials we have found Christ. These irksome duties and tasks became the turning point in our own lives and we exclaim in the end with the Psalmist: "For I shall yet praise Him" (Psalm 42:11).

II. THE DYING THIEF

Another confessor of Christ on Calvary was one of the malefactors, crucified with Jesus. We know little of his life's story. He had caused a sedition, irritated by the Roman occupation of his country. Every time he saw a Roman uniform his blood boiled within. Therefore he joined some zealous group which plotted the overthrow of the Roman powers. He had been unsuccessful, as many before him, and had to flee as a fugitive from the law. His food and keep came to him by theft and holdups. This made him a menace to society and his country. Finally he was caught and condemned to crucifixion.

The man may have started out with noble intentions and patriotic ideals, but he degenerated into a common robber against whom society and state had to be protected. So he was forcibly brought to Calvary and into the presence of Jesus. He witnessed all that happened and was done to the

Central Figure, next to him. He comes to Calvary as a criminal sinner, but before the sun sets over the western skies of Jerusalem he dies as a saint, saved by grace and goes to Paradise. In the last hour of his life he finds that peace which only Jesus can give, because He as Savior and Lamb of God died for the sin of the world. His eternity this thief is to spend in heaven. This all was his by the grace of God and by a faith created in his heart through the message of the cross.

Many start out in youth with high ideals in their hearts and yet make a mess of things. Life is hectic and disappointing. They find themselves hapless, helpless, and hopeless. Life has become a complete failure. Should they be left to despair? No, never! Even such, as they can come sobbing to the cross, crying out their heart in confession of sin, find in Jesus the Savior who promises healing and salvation. He can make the foulest clean. To each who comes to Him, Jesus promises Paradise. This is the assurance which our glorious Gospel gives to all.

III. THE CENTURION

Immediately after the darkness is lifted and Jesus is dead, the centurion steps forward and confesses that Jesus is the Son of God. This Roman officer was compelled by his call of duty to be at Calvary on that Friday. As he started that march to the hill with those three "criminals," he had no interest in these men except to have this "business" over before the sun would set. He was there on Calvary to see that his soldiers carried out the order of the governor. Therefore nothing escaped him. He heard Jesus' prayer for the soldiers—also the conversation between the three hanging on those crosses, and the promise this Jesus made to one of the men, a home in Paradise. He witnessed the three-hour darkness and felt the earthquake. He saw Jesus die and one of the soldiers pierce Him in the side. There on Calvary hatred and violence was seen in its crassest outbursts and, on the other hand, the calmness and kindliness of this Jesus. The centurion stands there alone, somewhat apart from the soldiers. He does not seek to share the loot of the garments nor take part in the dice-throwing. He abstains from mocking and jeering with the mob. He tried even to have the suffering of Jesus alleviated with hyssop. He stands on Calvary to wait the end. Seeing all and hearing all, the centurion passes judgment on the events which he had witnessed. In his own way he reverses the verdict of Pilate and the Jewish leaders. In him grew the conviction that Jesus was more than a righteous and good man. He was sure that this Jesus was the Son of God.

Tradition gives this centurion the name Longinus and says that he became a Christian. At least, there on Calvary he confessed: This Jesus *is* the Son of God.

This confession must be ours, too, at this very moment: Jesus is God. If we are to be certain of our personal salvation, then we *must* believe that Jesus is God of very God who has redeemed us from sin and damnation. If He is only man, even a righteous and sinless man, he could not redeem the world. Only the omnipotence of God could pay the satisfactory ransom for sin. So we must stand with the centurion at the cross and confess: Jesus is God, My God and My Savior.

IV. JOSEPH OF ARIMATHEA

On that Friday of the crucifixion of Jesus two latecomers arrived at Calvary and confessed: We belong. The one was Joseph of Arimathea. He hailed from the village where the prophet Samuel was born, called Ramah of old, then Arimathea, and by the historian Joseph Armatha. The place is about five miles north of Jerusalem. This Joseph had moved to the capital and had become a successful businessman. Matthew says he was rich and Mark calls him honorable. He had built for himself a fine tomb, which was not too far from Calvary.

Being prominent in Jerusalem, he had been voted into the Sanhedrin as layman. He had won the respect of the men of the priesthood and, therefore, was given this distinction. This Joseph believed in Jesus. However, he had not the courage on the day of condemnation to stand up for Jesus. He remained silent for fear of the Jews and kept the secret in his heart that he believed that Jesus was the Messiah.

After Jesus was dead, he came forward and identified himself with the crucified Galilean. He went to Pilate and told him that he belonged: This Jesus is my Friend. Therefore I want Him to have a decent burial. I have a sepulchre outside of the city wall, where I want to place His body. Pilate consented and Jesus was placed in the rich man's tomb. Therewith Isaiah's prophecy was fulfilled, to complete the cycle of prophetic statements which definitely designated this Jesus of Nazareth as the Messiah of God. Isaiah had said in his fifty third chapter that the Messiah would be "with the rich in His death." Still more important: By this act Joseph was instrumental in making sure the resurrection of Jesus. On the third day the sealed stone was rolled away. The women and the disciples, Peter and John, found the tomb empty and later saw the risen and living Christ who had died and was buried.

By boldly confessing Jesus as his Lord and Savior, Joseph of Arimathea rendered an outstanding service to the cause of the Gospel. So do we when we confess at every opportunity offered us: This Jesus is *my* Savior and *my* Lord.

V. NICODEMUS

The other latecomer to Calvary was Nicodemus. We meet him the first time that night when he stealthily and secretly came for an interview with Jesus. In this private talk Jesus told Nicodemus that great truth which has been repeated since by millions and millions of people the world over: "God so loved the world, that He gave His only begotten Son that whosoever believeth in Him should not perish but have everlasting life" (John 3:16). In that interview Jesus told this member of the Sanhedrin that he must be born again into the kingdom of God to be saved. He must look to Him who is crucified to have eternal life, even as the Israelites had to look up to the brazen serpent in Moses' day, if they should escape death. Nicodemus evidently was a timid man. He dared not come out openly for Jesus. He was present at the trial but had not the courage to be counted for the acquittal of Jesus. He was afraid of his associates in the assembly. He might lose some of the prestige he enjoyed. So he says nothing and he does nothing and lets Jesus go to Calvary.

However, after all is over and Jesus is dead, one of his associates of the Sanhedrin had come forward and asked for the body of Jesus. This gave Nicodemus courage and he joins Joseph of Arimathea in arranging the burial. He dares to come forward and identify himself with the crucified Messiah. He even provides the ointments needed to add to an honorable burial of Jesus.

To such like Nicodemus comes the urgent invitation: Come and confess Me! To such, even though they be latecomers, Jesus promises: I will confess them before My Father which is in heaven.

All Conditions of Men

As we stand on Calvary, in spirit, we see all types of men coming forward and identifying themselves with Jesus. We see the stranger from Africa coming along the road with no intention of interesting himself in the question: Is this Galilean the Christ? He is happy in his estate, finding himself contented in living and let live. Then something happens. Suddenly he is brought face to face with the biggest issue of his life: Christ Crucified! What shall I do with Him? With no desire to know Him, in no quest for the truth, he is unexpectantly confronted with Jesus and by the grace of God and through the power of the Holy Spirit he sees in this

Jesus *his* Savior. Blessed Simon!

We also see the sinner, whose gangsterism had brought him shame and humiliation and death, paying the bitter price of his transgression. He hangs on that cross, because society and the Law demands protection from evildoers of every type. In that last hour of his life, he is given one more chance. He is forced to hang there next to the Lamb of God who takes away all sin, also *his* sin. So his soul finds peace and heaven in Christ Jesus.

Then we see a Roman official, the centurion, whose duty, given him by the state, takes three men to Calvary to put them to death by a torturous crucifixion. His life has been hard and tough. He is keen and sharp, callous and realistic. Yet he cannot escape the fact that this Jesus *is* different. His gospel offers us something we find no other place in the world—a salvation by grace.

Once more, we look and see Joseph of Arimathea. He is a shrewd businessman. He does his thinking in terms of gold, sales, profits, and losses. He does his calculating and his speculating from the hilltops of expediency. The foremost question in his days asks: Does it pay? However, he too comes to realize that he gains nothing even if he gets all the finest pickings, should he lose his soul. He too discovers that it is Christ or nothing.

And finally we come to one influential leader of Jerusalem. He hobnobs with the elite and helps in shaping the destinies of the city. His name is found in *Who's Who*—well-bred, intellectual, with all the finesse and tact of the culture of the day. It is not easy to identify himself with the unpopular cause; to be linked to the zealous Prophet of Galilee. He was certain in his own mind that Jesus was more than a Prophet. But to say so, that was different. Eventually, after another associate of the Sanhedrin had the courage to step forward, Nicodemus too identifies himself with Jesus and pays tribute to Him as He is placed into Joseph's Tomb in Joseph's garden outside of the city.

At the present moment, we too are face to face with this question: What shall we do with Jesus, who is called the Christ? Perchance we too have been confronted with this Christ Crucified in an unusual and unique way. May *we* too in this very hour say:

> Beneath the Cross of Jesus
> This day I take my stand.

10

THE MIRACLES OF THE CROSS

"Now from the sixth hour there was a darkness over all
the land unto the ninth hour. Jesus, when He had cried
again with a loud voice, yielded up the ghost. And behold!
the veil of the Temple was rent in twain from the top
to the bottom; and the earth did quake, and the rocks
rent; And the graves were opened and many bodies of
the saints which slept arose, . . . and appeared unto many.
Now when the centurion, and they that were with him,
watching Jesus, saw the earthquake, and those things that
were done, they feared greatly, saying, Truly this was
the Son of God."—Matthew 27:45, 50-54.

The day that Jesus was crucified on Calvary and died before
the sun set in the western sky was one of the two greatest in
all history. The other day was His Resurrection day. On this
particular Friday of the Passover week was fought the most
decisive battle of the ages, and Jesus, the Messiah of God,
won. With this victory Jesus secured the redemption of all
mankind and made possible the salvation of all that are born
into this world. We, therefore, should not be surprised when
we read in the Gospel accounts that unusual events and dis-
turbances took place in the creation world. When Jesus died,
Who was the Maker of heaven and earth, the Lord of all died.
As Jesus cried with a loud voice: "It is finished," and bowed
His head and gave up His human life, strange and unique
happenings took place for which there is no natural explana-
tion. Neither can these events be brushed aside as coincidents:
The three-hour darkness, the rending of the veil in the
Temple, the earthquake, and the opening of the graves of

the saints who appeared at Jerusalem after Jesus' resurrection. These are miracles. They happened because Jesus died. For this reason they are to emphasize specific lessons to us. These miracles of the cross on that Good Friday deserve our careful attention, who have found our eternal peace through Calvary.

I. THE TOTAL DARKNESS

"Now from the sixth hour there was darkness over all the land unto the ninth hour." Since Matthew is addressing himself to Jewish Christians, he is using the Jewish reckoning of time. According to our time this darkness covered the land from twelve noon to three in the afternoon.

The nature of this darkness was unnatural. It could not have been an eclipse of the sun, for it lasted for three hours. A *total* eclipse of the sun lasts but a few minutes and is caused by the moon passing between the sun and the earth. Since the Passover always was observed during the week of full moon, this darkness was not caused by a natural eclipse of the sun. We have then a miraculous darkness which came on quickly and was so black that all those who stood on Calvary trembled and silently remained to see the end.

Is this account of the darkness true? Not only does Matthew tell us of this darkness in his Gospel, but also Mark and Luke. Matthew and Mark were at Jerusalem on that Friday. Then too, two of the prophets of the Old Testament foretold this miracle. Isaiah says in his fiftieth chapter, where he speaks of the Messiah: "I clothe the heavens in darkness, and I make sackcloth their covering." And Amos, living nearly eight hundred years prior to the crucifixion of Jesus, says in his eighth chapter: "And it shall come to pass in that day, saith the Lord God, that I will cause the sun to go down at noon, and I will darken the earth in a clear day." We also have a document, preserved for us by Tertulian, a Christian writer, born A.D. 150, who states: "At the moment of Christ's death the light departed from the sun and the land was darkened at noonday. Such wonder is related in your annals and is preserved in your archives to this day." This informs us that in the second century after Christ the account of this darkness could be found in the archive-records of Rome. We have no right, therefore, to question the truthfulness and the genuineness of this Matthew account.

But can we attach any significance to this darkness? The key is to be found in the next verse of Matthew's Gospel: "And about the ninth hour Jesus cried with a loud voice, saying, Eli, Eli, lama sabachthani? that is to say, My God, My God, why hast Thou forsaken Me?" Jesus was in the depth of His Passion, in the damnation of hell, and no human eye was to look on this agony. However, may we add that this darkness likewise emphasizes the blackness of sin. There is nothing so dreadful as the lost state of the soul as it goes out into the utter darkness of Satan's abode.

II. THE RENT VEIL

"And, behold, the veil of the Temple was rent in twain from the top to the bottom." This curtain hung between the Holy and the Most Holy in the Jerusalem Temple. This curtain was parted only once a year to allow the high priest to enter the Most Holy with a vessel of blood in his hands. This was to declare that blood had been shed for the sins committed against the holy will of God as revealed on Sinai. The fact that none but the high priest could enter the Holy of Holies, and that only with blood in his hands, was to tell mankind that sin closes the door to the presence of God. And sin could only be atoned for by the shedding of blood. "Without the shedding of blood, is no remission of sin" (Hebrews 9:22).

On the cross of Calvary, Jesus, the sinless Lamb of God, made a perfect sacrifice for sin. This was final and complete. So the veil was torn apart, to show that God is reconciled. No longer does a veil separate God from man. God looks at us through the cross and we are whiter than snow. Since there is remission of all sin through the Calvary sacrifice, there is no more offering or sacrifice for sin needed. So is written in the Epistle to the Hebrews in the tenth chapter. And what does this mean? This, that in the New Testament dispensation the sacrifice of lambs and bullocks is no longer necessary nor required. This ritual is done away with as Christ dies on Calvary. And since the sacrificial acts of the Temple are no longer to be offered, the priesthood passes out of the New Testament and only the prophet remains to proclaim to us this message of reconciliation. This the disciples understood. Immediately they do away with the Sabbath, the sacrifices of lambs and bullocks, the observances of the new moons, in fact, all the ceremonial rituals as they had been prescribed by Moses. Paul writes to the Colossians in 2:16, 17: "Let no man therefore judge you in meat, or in drink, or in respect of an holyday, or of the new moon, or of the sabbath days: which are a shadow of things to come; but the body is of Christ." Or as Phillips puts it in his *Letters to Young Churches:* "Don't let anyone worry you by criticising what you eat or drink, or what holy days you ought to observe, or bothering you over new moons or Sabbaths." Undoubtedly Jesus wants to stress this also to the Samaritan woman when He says in John 4:21, 23: "Woman, believe Me, the hour cometh, when ye shall neither in this mountain, nor yet at Jerusalem worship the Father. But the hour cometh, and now is, when the true worshippers shall worship the Father in spirit and in truth: for the Father seeketh such to worship Him."

The rent veil warns against the overemphasis of rituals and liturgy and stresses the simple approach to God to which every Christian is entitled as member of the priesthood of all believers. The rent veil declares that by faith each and every believer, without a priest, can come into the presence of God and speak to Him directly in prayer, through Christ Jesus who has redeemed us by this one sacrifice on Calvary.

"Where remission of these [sins] is, there is no more offering for sin" (Hebrews 10:18) .

III. THE EARTHQUAKE

"And the earth did quake, and the rocks rent." This happened soon after Jesus Christ cried aloud: "It is finished!" and bowed His head in death. The Lord of the universe dies and the earth trembles and the rocks are torn apart. But *the cross still stands*. This did not topple over and fall to the ground. This, too, is a miracle which wants to proclaim to us that the gates of hell did not succeed against the Lord's Anointed.

Yet the trembling earth sobs and shakes as the Lord of all creation dies. All the universe is affected by Jesus' death. And the people who witnessed and felt the earthquake smote on their breasts and were filled with fear. Did many think that the world was coming to an end? Perhaps so! Of old the smiting on the breast was a sign of the terrifying consequence of sin. Sin upsets our human composure and in the end drives us into despair. Sin condemns and convicts us, especially, in days when great upheavals take place in nature. Floods, tornadoes, fires, epidemics, earthquakes awaken many to the realization that we have sinned terribly and often. However, you and I, as children of God's grace, know that we cannot perish eternally, no matter how many earthquakes and catastrophies come upon us. The cross stands as the eternal surety that no one can pluck us out of His pierced hands. As sin does its worst, Christ lifts us to His wounded side and His loving heart to give us hope, peace, and heaven.

IV. THE OPENED GRAVES OF THE SAINTS

"And the graves were opened, and many bodies of the saints which slept arose and came out of the graves after His resurrection, and went into the holy city, and appeared to many." The graves of the saints were opened. These were the sepulchres of Old Testament believers, who were looking for the

Messiah. These, who had been placed into those graves, some many years before, arose bodily and appeared in the city of Jerusalem to many. These appearances seem to have been of the same nature as that of Christ *after* His resurrection. The same Greek word is used, which is used when speaking of the appearances of Jesus to His disciples and others. These saints, then appeared with a "glorified" body like that of Jesus, the risen Lord.

What was the significance of this miracle of the cross? Christ died that we might have life, a life that is eternal, and this miracle proclaimed that death had been conquered and the resurrection of our body is a fact. This our body is after all incorruptible and indestructible. Our confession of faith, "I believe in the resurrection of the body and life everlasting," is more than wishful thinking. A glorious truth is proclaimed which dries our tears as we stand at open graves. On the other side of the grave is life eternal, where saints are in glory. Here is the answer to the oft-repeated question: "If a man die, shall he live again?"

This miracle is God's *Yes.*

V. THE MIRACLE OF CONVERSION

"I, if I be lifted up, will draw all men unto Me." So said Jesus to the multitude after His triumphal entry into Jerusalem. His sacrifice on the cross is to change the hearts of men. This same truth Jesus emphasized the night Nicodemus came to interview the Galilean Prophet secretly. "As Moses lifted up the serpent in the wilderness, even so must the Son of man be lifted up, That whosoever believeth in Him should not perish, but have eternal life" (John 3:14, 15). Is this true? Let us see!

A thief hangs on another cross nearby. He is an outcast of society. He himself admits that he is no good. He deserves what he is getting. So sin has done its worst to him and life is ebbing out in disgust and despair. In that last hour he looks to Jesus and is promised heaven with all its glory.

Dead in sin, he is made alive and a new creature with peace in his heart and hope for tomorrow. A miracle has taken place. Christ has lifted the thief to His heart and washed and healed him from the blackest of his sins. Only the Crucified can create a clean heart and make sinners into reborn children of His grace.

However, a centurion also stands at the cross and witnesses all that is taking place on Calvary. He is a man of the world. He has been around and seen many things and been in many places. He has kept himself of good report. He has risen from the ranks to be a centurion and moved well in officialdom of the Roman Empire. Pontius Pilate had given him a "chore" to do. He was to supervise the crucifixion of three "criminals." As he was awaiting their end, he stood on Calvary and saw all that was happening. His attention was riveted on Him who hung on the central cross and had prayed for those who were nailing Him to the tree. He heard Jesus promise Paradise to one of the other evildoers and saw His solicitous commitment of His mother to John who stood with her beneath the cross. He saw the darkness and witnessed the earthquake. As he did his callous heart was touched and a conviction grew in him that this Man, designated as the King of the Jews, was more than a man and more than a pretender of the Jewish kingdom. Certainly He was not a criminal as were the other two. He saw nobility of character. This man is righteous. He saw more. He was sure that he saw God. To die as this Man dies, He must be God. And so the centurion confessed: "Truly this was the Son of God!" So this army man is drawn to the Christ, uplifted on the cross, and made over into a child of grace. He, too, believes that this Jesus is his God and his Savior. This truly is a miracle of the cross.

Today's Miracle

This last miracle of that Good Friday goes on day after day in all parts of the world. Men and women are reborn and created anew into believers of the cross. This miracle of being a Christian is the greatest which comes from that cross. Through the power of the Holy Spirit you and I also have been made into children of God, lifted to the heart of Christ Jesus to be His own in time and in heaven. Only this Calvary sacrifice of the Lamb of God could do this mighty deed. Without this shedding of blood our sins still would stand against us to condemn us throughout all eternity.

The miracles of the cross, as you and I well see, are not meaningless incidents. They proclaim the power and the victory of the cross, the wonder of the cross, the salvation of the cross. No wonder Paul exclaims: "I am not ashamed of the Gospel of Christ for it is a *power* of God unto salvation to every one that believeth" (Romans 1:16).

Today you and I are asked to stand at the side of the thief and the centurion to confess Jesus as the Son of God and our Savior. Here is forgiveness; here is salvation. If we confess Him who died on Calvary as our Savior, He will confess us also before His Father in heaven and claim us as His own. Knowing this we can go forth from this place of worship with *peace* in our heart, our *mind* at ease, our *hopes* high, and our heavenly mansions assured. Today

> Two wonders we confess
> The wonders of His glorious love
> And our own worthlessness.

11

THE REVELATION OF THE CROSS

"For God so loved the world, that He gave His only begotten Son, that whosoever believeth in Him should not perish, but have everlasting life."—John 3:16.

Change and decay, wars and depressions, outer space satellites and missiles, sickness and death cannot destroy the fact of Calvary. *The cross still stands* as the hope of the world, proclaiming to confused and fear haunted man reconciliation with God through His only begotten Son. When the world was created in the beginning of time, the angels sang the morning hymn; when the Babe of Bethlehem was born the angelic host came down from heaven to sing the Glory Song; but when Jesus died on Calvary darkness covered the earth. Yet out of that utter blackness of night came the greatest proclamation in all history: God is reconciled to man through the cross of His Son.

At the present moment we want to ponder upon this revelation of the cross, a revelation so amazing and so astounding that it has become the greatest news release of the ages, a *Gospel* for all mankind. Since this revelation was made no one need ever despair. At Calvary we receive the ultimatum: *Christ* or *nothing.* Thousands and ten thousands of American homes are happier to-day. In Europe as well as in Asia and far off Australia and New Zealand men and women, young and old, everybody, lift up their heads with hope in the heart because of this revelation of the cross.

I. THE GREATEST REVELATION OF THE CROSS

The greatest revelation ever made to man is couched in four one-syllable words: *God loved the world.* This revelation came to man from God Himself. This truth God proclaimed through His Son, and made it known to us and all mankind through the Gospel.

This revelation takes God for granted. The Bible says that it is self-evident that God is. "The heavens declare the glory of God" and the greatness of Jehovah. Only the fool says: "There is no God." In your home stands a table and some chairs. They are made of wood. That wood once was a tree. How did that tree become a chair? Certainly not by itself. Some intelligence made the tree into a chair. I cannot say, by looking at the chair, what kind of person made the chair, whether white or black, young or old, American or foreign-born; but of this I am sure that an intelligent human being made the chair. I can take that for granted. In like manner the revelations of Scripture take God for granted. But *how God feels* toward me and what His name may be is not written across the sky or carved into the bark of the tree. God Himself must reveal His feelings and His attitude toward us and tell us His name. This God had done in the Bible, His revelations of Himself.

God says: He loved. This love was unselfish and is sacrificial. It is an all-embracing love; love to the fullest. God says of Himself: *He is love.* This love God showed to the world. What is meant by *"the world"*? The "world" in this instance is the world of human people who live on this earth. There are other "worlds." We speak of the animal world, of the starry world, of the physical world. This love, however, is bestowed only on the world of man. God loved and loves people.

This human world is in pain. These people have heart-aches, sickness, disappointments. They are driven into doubt, hopelessness, and despair. Sin has done this to man. Nothing worse has come upon man than sin. It has separated man from God. Sin brought in its train suffering of body, mind, and spirit. As God sees this suffering of sinful man, He is filled with a divine pity and wants to help. God loves.

This people is in tears. Sin has put death at our doors of life. Daily death is taking its toll. Death takes the fathers who are breadwinners, mothers who are so needed for the smooth running of the family, sons and daughters who are the joy of life, and sweethearts and friends. Life becomes lonely, meaningless, and empty. God sees all this and His love wants to help these people by drying their tears and putting a new hope into their hearts.

This people live in sin. Day after day we displease God by our disobedience and our rebellious spirit. Sin offends God, insults God, defies God. God hates sin with a perfect hatred but loves the sinner and does not want any of us to perish. Such is His love.

God tells us that He loves the world. This love is personal and direct. We belong to the whole world, but God loves each one of us as an individual person. God does not think of us in terms of nations, communities, generations, and families. God thinks of us as John, Henry, Mary, and Susan. Because of this personalized love for us we are better than a sheep.

To this love there is no limit or limitation. That is why Jesus says to Nicodemus: "God *so* loved the world." There is no word in our human speech which can adequately define the height, the depth, the width, and the breadth of God's love. It cannot be measured or weighed. It is so marvelous, so far-reaching in its importance that we cannot evaluate it with a word or many words.

Here then we have the greatest revelation of the ages: *God loved the world.*

II. THE GREATEST DEMONSTRATION OF
THIS REVELATION

How did God reveal this love? "He gave His only begotten

Son." God *gave*. This was a gift of love. Long before you and I were born and lived, God gave His Son, who gave His life on Calvary that you and I might have a hope and a peace right now. We have done nothing to merit this love. It is a gift. God was under no obligation to us to love us. And as He gave and demonstrated this love to us He attached no strings to the gift, as we commonly say. It was an outright gift of love, available even to those who spurn the gift and smite God in the face, yes, deny the very existence of God. However, all this did not deter God from making the gift. God knew that millions upon millions would not appreciate this gift, much less accept it, *yet God gave*, readily, unstintingly, with all His heart and with all His Being.

And what did God give? *His Son*, His only Son, the only One born as Son. God has other children. God calls you and me sons and daughters. However, we are adopted and engrafted, not born as sons. But this Son Jesus, whom God gave in His love, is His only begotten Son, "God of very God, begotten, not made, being of one substance with the Father," as we confess in the Nicene Creed.

This Son, Jesus, has been Son from all eternity. Long before He was born of the Virgin Mary, made flesh, is He the Son, the Christ, the Messiah, the Anointed of the Lord. In the fullness of time this Christ-Messiah became flesh and dwelt among us. At that time He was given a *human* name: Jesus. The boys of Nazareth with whom He played called Him *Jesus*. However, God in heaven told Mary to name Him *Jesus*, for "He shall save His people from their sins." In this Son we behold the fullness of God and we behold a true man, sinless, as Adam was in the beginning when he came from the creative hands of God. This is the mystery that our human mind cannot fathom.

And *why* did God give His Son Jesus Christ just in this way, "true God begotten of the Father from all eternity, and also true man, born of the Virgin Mary"? God gave Him into this world that Jesus might redeem man from sin, death, and Satan. As mere man, even though sinless, He could not do this. This redemption required the omnipotence of God. No other power could crush the serpent's head and release mankind from the damnation of hell. This Jesus *must* be God to redeem. However, "as God of very God" He could not shed blood and "without the shedding of blood there is no remission of sin." So Jesus was born flesh of flesh of the Virgin Mary and as man ate, drank, slept, wearied, suffered, and even died. As He died on Calvary's cross His human *blood* was shed.

In the giving of His only begotten Son, God gave the greatest demonstration of this revelation that He loved the world.

III. THE TERMINUS OF THIS REVELATION

And *what* good was to come forth from this Son's death on Calvary? "That whosoever believeth in Him should not perish, but have everlasting life." That is the purpose of the death: To give believers a life without end. This is great news, for we all love life and want to live. With Ponce de Leon we all are looking for the fountain of youth. Natively we do not want to die. However, Paul the Apostle longs to die. And why? That He might be with Christ forever. Only the Christian wants to die, but not to end all. He wants to die to go to a fuller and richer and a most perfect life. The believer wants to pass through death to live forever in the presence of His Savior who died for him on Calvary.

The revelation of God tells us Christians that the terminus of the believer is eternal life. To make this possible God gave His Son. That Son gave Himself on the cross for the world, whom He loved. However, this terminus of life eternal is reached only by believers of the cross. So says God in His revelations. The believer who reaches eternal life believes *four* foremost truths through this revelation of God's love.

The believer believes that Jesus Christ took our sin to His Calvary and atoned, made good, by paying the ransom price of redemption with His own blood. Each believer says: Jesus died *for me* on that cross.

Then the believer believes that the perfect holiness or righteousness of Jesus covers the believer's unrighteousness and sinfulness so completely that God sees no more sin in us. To Him we are "whiter than snow" as we stand beneath the cross.

Thirdly, the believer, living in grace, has none of his sin counted against him. "There is therefore now no condemnation to them which are in Christ Jesus, who walk not after the flesh, but after the Spirit" (Romans 8:1). The believer is certain that he lives continually in the sunshine of God's love, forgiven of all sin, to live in Christ and Christ in him.

And finally the believer believes and knows that heaven is his home where he shall stand before the throne of the Lamb to praise Him world without end and that in a fullness of joy.

"Whosoever"

What is the name of this believer who is so sure? His name is *Whosoever*.

This world cheats and steals, hates and murders, commits the most brutal acts, defies and even curses God, but God's love and God's gift is for the thief and the murderer, the unbeliever, and the atheist. Paul writes to the Corinthians: "That God was in Christ, reconciling the world unto Himself, not imputing their trespasses unto them; and hath committed unto us the word of reconciliation" (2 Corinthians 5:19). However, only those who believe that Christ died for them on the cross receive the benefits of this love and are saved. The thief believed this. To him Jesus therefore says: "Today—with Me—in Paradise." This WHOSOEVER included this dying thief. That is what the revelation of God says. God loves and gives regardless of what the world does to Him who is so gracious and full of compassion.

Christians in many places and under circumstances deny the Savior, are ashamed of Jesus, ignore the Gospel call, but God's love and God's gift is also for them and so Simon Peter is included in the WHOSOEVER.

The self-righteous are offended if they are called sinners. They boast that they are so much better than the mill-run of people. They need no Savior. They can take care of themselves. They think that they can demand heaven, for they "lack nothing." God knows better and His love and patience pleads and the Holy Spirit opens their eyes to see their lovelessness, their selfishness, which makes them look with contempt on others. These who are proud in heart are also included in the WHOSOEVER. So Paul comes and confesses: "This is a faithful saying and worthy of all acceptation, that Christ Jesus came into the world to save sinners; of whom I am chief" (1 Timothy 1:15).

That WHOSOEVER also includes you and me. "Him that cometh unto me I will in no wise cast out" (John 6:37). "There is neither Jew nor Greek, there is neither bond nor free, there is neither male nor female; for ye are all one in Christ Jesus" (Galatians 3:28). God loves ALL in Christ. In this respect God makes no distinction in race, color, age, or prestige. Some in this world and in the community are men, others women, some are white, others black, some are young, others old. There are differences. No one denies this. A man is not a woman biologically. But whether man or woman, God loves them; both are included in the *Whosoever of the Cross*.

These believers of the cross cannot perish, says this great revelation of God. No matter what befalls them in this life, heaven is their eternal home. God does not promise them immunity from the woes of life, sickness, pain, hunger, financial losses, even physical death, but for them life eternal is guaranteed. This life begins now. As we come to faith by the creative power of the Holy Spirit we become alive in Christ *spiritually* and live in the grace of God. "And you hath he quickened [made alive], who were dead in trespasses and sins" (Ephesians 2:1). That is why Peter says: "Being born again, not of corruptible seed, but of incorruptible, by the Word of God, which liveth and abideth forever" (1 Peter 1:23). This dust-me is indestructible, for we shall rise from the dead to be with Him who is risen from the dead on that first Easter morn. This is the promise to *whosoever believeth* in Him.

There is no greater revelation in all the world. The spotlight of the ages is therefore focused on that cross. Here is Gospel! The cross reveals a love "so amazing, so divine" that it includes you and me. What more can we ask?

> O wondrous love to bleed and die
> To bear the guilt and shame
> That guilty sinners such as I
> Might plead His gracious name.

12

THE CLAIMS OF THE CROSS

*"For it pleased the Father that in Him should
all fullness dwell; and, having made peace
through the blood of the cross, by Him to
reconcile all things unto Himself; by Him, I say,
whether they be things in earth, or things
in heaven. And you, that were sometime
alienated and enemies in your mind by
wicked works, yet now hath He reconciled
In the body of His flesh through death,
to present you holy and unblamable
and unreprovable in His sight."*
—Colossians 1:19-22.

"In the cross of Christ I glory"—do we? Are we identifying ourselves at all times with Christ Jesus? Do our friends
say that our loyalties ring true and do the enemies of the
cross admire us for our convictions?

Do we ourselves know what the cross of Christ means to us
and to the world in which we live? Would our community be
different if none of us had ever heard of the cross and the
significance of its message? Has the Gospel added anything
to our outlook on life and the hope of our future?

Let us retrace for a moment our steps to the year A.D. 1.
As we do, we find ourselves in the golden age of the Roman
Empire, which as a nation had reached the heights of its
glory. Augustus had ruled for nearly fifty years and his accomplishments as emperor of Rome had made the nation
the envy and the power of the world.

Some of the greatest minds had given their best to the

world, a literature which still serves as models to modern man. Some of the foremost artists of the ages had lived and produced some of the greatest works and architects vied with one another in giving the empire some magnificent buildings, such as Herod's Temple and the Diana Temple at Ephesus. It was Rome's golden age.

However, that period of marvelous achievements could not boast of any hospitals for the general public, had no orphanages for the fatherless children, no home for the aged. Most people of the realm never attended school, could neither read nor write. The city of Rome had more than 200,000 slaves, who had no rights, nor could appeal their case to any court: and crucifixion often was the means of putting them and the evildoers to death. Sometimes more than a thousand would be crucified at one time.*

About the year A.D. 30 of our reckoning, one Jesus was crucified outside of the walls of Jerusalem. That crucifixion changed the world. The death of Jesus on Calvary's tree did something to the race of man. *That is the claim of the cross.*

I. THE WORLD NEEDS A MESSIAH

The cross claims that the human race needs a Messiah, sent from God, to save the souls of mankind. The world is not able to free itself from the forces of evil and the powers of wickedness. The trend of humanity is toward wrongdoing and sin. "Out of the heart proceed evil thoughts." If any

---

*Gerhard Uhlorn, *Conflict of Christianity with Heathenism,* published 1879, says that there was some charity in paganism toward the needy and some compassion; "what, however, was wanting was a regulated and systematic benevolence" (p. 195).

"Hospitals existed only for soldiers, gladiators and slaves. The manual laborer who was without means, the poor man who was not a slave, found no place of refuge. . . . Men feared death and took no interest in their own sick, but drove them out of the house and left them to their fate. The ancient world was a world without love" (p. 196). See also Steward Perowne, *The Later Herods,* Chapter III: The War of Varus.

peace is to be made with God, the Lord Himself must write the peace treaty. God has done this by coming in His Son into the world and to reconcile Himself through the blood of the cross, for in Christ Jesus dwells the fullness of God. Jesus is the Promised Messiah who was wounded for our transgressions that we might be healed and restored to grace.

This the world could not do. The world uses its facilities selfishly. Much of its technical knowledge is used "to beat the other fellow at the game" of destruction. One group seeks to advance itself at the expense of the other with a definite lag and unawareness of spiritual values. Men and women are used as steppingstones for our own ambitions. We cannot deny that many of our inventions have benefited humanity. In wide areas of human endeavor the inventions in the technical field have lightened the burdens of the day. However, we must admit that many of our inventions have been channeled into fields where whole nations are submerged and even destroyed.

Again, mankind uses its discoveries of natural resources to take from others what they possess. We need but read history to substantiate this. Greed and self-aggrandizement have been the causes of war, invasions, captivities. The Golden Rule becomes a secondary precept in the thinking of human society. The race of men needs help, help from without and from above. The Word must become flesh and dwell among us. So God sent His Messiah in Christ.

Rosters of Achievements Do Not Save

However, this need does not become apparent to unbelieving and sinful man. He thinks he can take care of himself. Man points to his achievements and the advancements he has made in the various fields of science and education. And we must admit that the roster is impressive. The performances in the technical area have given us a better country in which to live. However, all this has not made the heart of man better and nobler. We still are born in sin and are by nature selfish, unclean, spiteful, and deceitful.

The cross of Jesus exposes this selfishness, which leads to pride, greed, lovelessness, race distinction, cast systems. The cross focuses the light on the brutality of the superman and the heartlessness of the self-righteous. In the light of the cross there is none that doeth good and sinneth not.

The Cross Holds Out Hope

The cross of Jesus does not stop here, telling man of his inherited sinfulness. The cross offers help. Jesus holds out His pierced hands of Calvary and draws mankind to His heart and gives all a new hope. "And I, if I be lifted up from the earth, will draw all men unto Me" (John 12:32). God sent His Messiah into this world to make even the social and community living better. As the Gospel changes the heart of many, the community improves. The more believers of the cross live in a city, the better the community will be. By putting some of the love of Christ into our hearts, we learn to live peaceably with one another. Each changed heart realizes that every other person in the community has a soul, redeemed by Christ, and must be told of this Jesus and should be won for Him. We are our brother's keeper. We must lift our hands and assist in bettering conditions around us. We are not only concerned about better living conditions but, above all, about the souls of men whom Christ has purchased with His own blood.

However, too many repudiate the claim of the cross. Even many of us, who profess to be followers of Christ are indifferent and lukewarm and thus retard the growth of the church. The cross demands and claims our first loyalty and devotion. The Gospel of this cross puts love into our hearts, fills us with compassion for the troubled and needy, and with kindness toward those who walk with us the Jericho road of life. This will only be the case, however, if Jesus is our Messiah and we as His people realize that we need Him to lead richer and fuller lives.

II. YOU NEED A SAVIOR

The cross furthermore claims that *you* personally need a Savior. You and I have failed to attain to that ideal for which we are in this world, that is, to do completely and altogether the will of God and live to His glory. This does not imply that we were out last night to rob a bank or this afternoon to snatch women's purses. However, we have not lived in that perfect holiness in which man was created in the beginning of time and in that sinlessness which is in Christ Jesus.

Our failures may be those of Saul, who was to become Paul. In his community he was highly esteemed. He believed in observing the Law and would not stoop to do anything which public opinion disapproved. He would not accept a bribe, slander his neighbor, fail to pay his tithe. Yet there was something radically wrong with him. His zeal was misdirected, his concept of salvation false, his refusal to accept Jesus as Messiah a sin which closed to him the door to the eternal mansions. Later in life, after the Damascus experience, he realized how far he had erred from the way, and calls himself in sincere humility *the chief* among sinners. Too often we think we are good enough to take care of our salvation and demand heaven because of our accomplishments and good behavior.

Or ours may be the sins of Peter. He professed to be a follower of Jesus. He had made one of the noblest confessions of faith. In the Upper Room he insisted that he even would die for Christ. But the moment that he was out of sight of his friends and face to face with those who were warming themselves at the fires of opposition, he tried to get down to the sinful level of the cursing and foul-mouthed soldiers and hide his identity. No one would suspect him to be a disciple of Jesus as they watched his conduct that night in the patio of Caiaphas. Later he realized what he had done and went out and wept bitterly. He, too, needed a Savior. The sin of denial is a sin of a Christian. And must we not confess that too often we fail to let people know that we belong to Him, who hangs on that accursed tree. We, too, need the Savior and His compassionate forgiveness.

Or our failures may be like those of John. John was one of the saintliest of Jesus' disciples. He dared to stand under the cross and say: I belong. Yet standing beneath that cross, John realized that the holiness which is in Jesus is not found in him. Even he is a sinner. Later John confesses: "If we say that we have no sin, we deceive ourselves, and the truth is not in us" (1 John 1:8). Even John needed a Savior. So do you and I. In us is not to be found that perfect holiness, sinlessness, which was in Christ Jesus.

No one can stand in the presence of the cross and say: I can take care of myself. The cross claims that we all need a Savior, who alone can wash, cleanse, and heal us from our sins, keep us in grace, and give us eternal life. Each one of us must confess:

> Nothing in my hands I bring,
> Simply to Thy cross I cling.

III. THE ONLY WAY TO LIFE

The cross claims that the death of Jesus on Calvary was the only means by which man could be reconciled to God. "And having made peace through the blood of the cross, by Christ to reconcile all things to Himself," that is, to God. The death of Jesus met the requirements of God's holiness. This death paid the penalty for sin. God had said to Adam in the garden. "In the day that thou eatest thereof thou shalt surely die" (Genesis 2:17). With Adam's disobedience sin and death came into the world and upon all of the human race. However, God also promised Adam who had sinned that He would send a Savior who would redeem and release the sinner from the power and dominion and curse of sin. This redemption came to us through the shedding of Christ's blood on Calvary.

This death revealed God's amazing concern and love for

us. He did not want us to perish. God was willing to send
His Son and this Son Jesus was ready to leave His heavenly
abode, become flesh, and dwell among men, to fulfill the
Law of Sinai for us by His perfect holiness and then take
upon Himself the iniquity of us all and redeem us with
His own precious blood.

Love and Justice Meet in the Cross

By this act the holiness and the love of God merged to
make a satisfactory and complete reconciliation. The Law
was fulfilled and the sinner set free from the penalty of
death. By this sacrifice of Calvary's Christ we are presented
to God holy, unblamable, and unreprovable.

Holy, because all our sin is hid from God as He beholds
us through the cross. Clothed in the righteousness-holiness of
Jesus, we are whiter than snow.

Unblamable, because Jesus took upon Himself the full
blame of our transgressions.

Unreprovable, because nothing remains undone. The debt
is paid in full.

On the one hand, then, we are accused of transgressing the
Sinai law of God and our conscience testifies against us; but,
on the other hand, Jesus steps in and assumes the full guilt
and by faith we stand beneath the cross to be acquitted. So
the cross claims that there is no condemnation in them that
are in Christ Jesus. We have a Savior. He is the *only* Savior
who can free the souls of men from eternal damnation.

IV. IN CHRIST MADE NEW CREATURES

And then—the cross claims that this sacrificial death of
Jesus transforms the whole life and being of those who believe. Our status has changed. We were aliens, but now we
are citizens; we were sinners, but now we are saints; we were
slaves, but now we are children of the household. We are
living in grace, continually and always forgiven and washed
and cleansed. We bask in the sunshine of God's love and

enjoy a security that goes beyond this life into heaven. That is what Paul wants to stress, when he says: "To present you holy, and unblamable, and unreprovable."

Our *attitudes* are changed. We are co-workers with God. We seek to co-operate in all that God wills in Christ. From doubt and suspicion we turn to trust and confidence. We know that nothing can separate us from the love of God which He has for us in Christ Jesus. We have a security that makes us secure. We cannot perish, even when we pass through many trials and troubles in this present world.

Our *life* is changed. The moment that Paul became a Christian, he asked: "Lord, what wilt Thou have me to do?" He realized that his life must be devoted to the cause of his Savior who had given His life's blood on the cross that he might have that peace that passeth understanding, that hope which never fades, that salvation which is certain and sure. To this Christ Jesus, Paul desired to dedicate his life.

This must be our aim as children of God's family. Transparently sincere, we dedicate our life to the services of our Savior and that in joyful obedience. All that we say and do indicates that we belong to Jesus. Loving Him, we are ready to make sacrifices for His cause. We will work in His vineyard; we will bear witness to Him who gave His life for our redemption; we will consecrate our all, our time, our talents, our possessions, our love to Him without whom we have no hope.

The cross claims that all this we will do in sincere appreciation to Him who has delivered us from the guilt of sin and the fear of death and given us life eternal.

V. NO OTHER SOLUTION TO LIFE'S ILLS

The cross claims, finally, that we have no alternative, no other solution to the ills of life. We have Christ or nothing. Without the cross of Christ we perish. "He that believeth not shall be damned" (Mark 16:16) . "Neither is there salvation in any other: for there is none other name under heaven

given among men, whereby we must be saved" (Acts 4:12).
We cannot find peace at Sinai. The Law says: Do this and
thou shalt live. But we all have fallen short of doing the
will of God. No matter how much we try, we fail, for we are
born in sin, with a sinful nature. Nothing unclean shall
enter the kingdom. At the cross we are cleansed, for the
blood of Jesus Christ His Son cleanses us from *all* sin. And
whosoever believes this cannot perish. One thing Almighty
God cannot do, condemn the sinner who stands under the
cross. This is the claim of the cross of Calvary.

Without the cross of Christ we despair. There is no hope
for any who demand salvation on the plea of doing the will
of God. God demands more than an outward obedience. Not
only he who kills and steals transgresses the commandment,
but also he who hates and covets. So our case is hopeless
unless we look to the cross. But beneath the cross is certain
salvation. There the dying thief found heaven; there David
found forgiveness; there Zacchaeus found peace; there Paul
found heaven's door opened.

Without the cross and its healing power we perish. But
none need go to destruction. The cross claims that it is
able to make the foulest clean. Under the cross of Jesus we
can claim exemption from the condemning judgments of
God. Standing at that cross, God looks at us through this
cross and sees none of our sins, because the robe of Jesus'
holiness and righteousness covers us altogether.

This is the claim of the cross: That him who comes Christ
Jesus will not cast out. So I come. Will you?

> Just as I am, without one plea
> But that Thy blood was shed for me
> And that Thou bidst me come to Thee,
> O Lamb of God, I come.

13

THE BLOOD OF THE CROSS

> *"When Pilate saw that he could prevail nothing, but that rather a tumult was made, he took water, and washed his hands before the multitude, saying, I am innocent of the blood of this just person: see ye to it. Then answered all the people, and said, His blood be on us, and our children."*—Matthew 27:24, 25.

More than 1900 years ago a man was crucified whose name is spoken with great reverence by millions and millions of people in all parts of the world. This countless number has found in Jesus the one and only hope in a world of sin, destruction, and despair. However, tens of thousands in an inexplicable bitterness of heart reject Him and with defiance on their lips and scorn in their eyes have gone to their doom in a hopelessness from which there is no escape.

The day that Jesus was crucified outside of the walls of Jerusalem the hours were packed with fast-moving events. At sunrise of that signal Friday the Temple officials and the leaders of the Sanhedrin brought Jesus, bound, to Pontius Pilate, who that year was governor of Judea and Samaria, appointed by the Roman Senate. Roman Law did not permit the Sanhedrin to pronounce the death sentence which the Jewish leaders wanted for Jesus of Nazareth. Seemingly helpless, this Jesus stands before the Roman judge, yet He is the One who gave the world the Gospel which broke the cruel, brutal power of Rome.

Pilate's Court

Pontius Pilate had taken quarters at the Herodian palace,

which had been built by Herod the Great and was one of the show places in Jerusalem. The main dome was in blue, studded with golden stars. To this palatial residence Jesus was brought that Pontius Pilate might pronounce upon the Nazarene the death sentence by crucifixion. The governor appears on the elevation, called Gabbatha, to face the tumultuous crowd of excited people. He asks: What accusation bring you against this man?* Defiantly the leaders reply: If He were not a malefactor, we would not have brought him here to you! To this Pilate replied: If He is such, take Him, and judge Him according to your law. To this the Sanhedrin men reply: You know as well as we, that we have no right to put Him to death. And that is what we want, a death sentence.

Pilate then proceeds to hear the case, asking the leaders what charge they are bringing against this Jesus. Three accusations they make in this Roman court:

1. We found Him perverting the nation; He is undermining the state.
2. He is telling the people to refuse to pay their state tax.
3. He claims to be the Anointed of God, a king, who wants to set up the throne of king David. He even insists that He is a legal descendant of our famous king.

Hearing these accusations, the governor dares not ignore their implications. Therefore he orders the prisoner to the judgment hall to be tried.

In the courtroom Pilate questions Jesus. After a time, the governor appears again on the Gabbatha, for the Jews would not go into the courtroom. Doing so they would defile themselves and this would bar them from the Passover meal. That is why Pilate has to come out to them to announce his decision: I find no fault in this man whatsoever. At once the group is in an uproar. All shout at once, the one this, the other that. A tumult and riot is in the making. Emotions run wild, fists

---

*The Scripture texts are paraphrased and follow no standard version in this sermon.

are clenched, threats are heard. If you let this man go, you are not Caesar's friend, and we shall report so.

During this time Jesus stands there in silence, calm and composed. Pilate notes that Jesus gives no backtalk. So he turns to the prisoner, saying: Do you not answer? Listen! how many things they say against you! But Jesus remains silent. He refuses to comment. So both, Pilate and Jesus, stand on the elevation, facing the turbulent mob, which is becoming more violent moment to moment. The leaders want action. With insistence they claim: He stirs up the people. He is dangerous to public safety. His doctrine is pernicious. Everywhere people are following Him in ever larger number, not only here but above all in Galilee. Are you a Galilean? asks Pilate as he turns to Jesus. Jesus replies that He is.

From Pilate to Herod

At once Pilate sees a way out for himself. Galilee is under the jurisdiction of Herod Antipas and Herod is in the city for the Passover. Then and there Pilate decides to "pass the buck" as we commonly say and sends Jesus to the Galilean ruler. Off the soldiers go to Herod's quarters with their prisoner Jesus. The howling mob follows.

Herod welcomes the opportunity of seeing Jesus. He had heard a good deal of the Prophet in his domain. This Jesus had raised the youth at Nain from the dead; He had opened the eyes of some of the blind in his realm; He had even cleansed lepers from their loathesome disease. So went the report. Herod, somewhat bored with the Passover routine, is glad to see Jesus. He hopes Jesus will do something unusual. This will break the monotony of the day. However, to all of Herod's questions Jesus answers not a word. The leaders continue with their accusations, different from those made to Pilate, for Herod is one of their own. They charge: He says that He is the Son of God. He wants to be the Messiah. He even says He can destroy our temple, built by our fathers, and that He will build a new one in three days. To all this Jesus answers not a word. Herod sees through it all. Therefore, he says to himself: This Man is harmless! Why should I get involved in this case? He has enough problems of his own. So Herod orders a gorgeous robe put on Him, which tradition says was white, as an evidence of Jesus' innocence. Then Herod sends Jesus back to Pilate. He will not pronounce the death sentence.

Once more Pontius Pilate has Jesus on his hands. The governor appears again on Gabbatha and tells the restless crowd that he has not sufficient evidence for the conviction of Jesus. I find him not guilty of the things of which you accuse Him. Neither does Herod, who knows your laws better than I do. However, to satisfy you, I will put Him to the whipping post and have Him scourged. Then I will let Him go. The mob grows furious. They threaten. Their shouting becomes more vehement. With that Pilate is handed a note and reads: Have nothing to do with this just Man. I have suffered many things during this night in a dream about Him. Signed: Procula. The note is from Pilate's wife. Pilate, being superstitious as many Romans were, is uneasy and perturbed.

Jesus or Barabbas

Pilate has another happy thought, he believes. According to Passover custom a prisoner is to be released. A flash comes to his mind—Barabbas. That is the man! Pilate is going to place Barabbas next to Jesus. He feels certain that this Barabbas will never be chosen. He is too dangerous a man and everybody is afraid of him. He has terrorized the country and all are happy that he is in jail. Everybody feels safer. This incorrigible man the governor has brought to the Gabbatha and placed next to Jesus. Then Pilate says to the mob: Take your choice!

The leaders are stunned but not "licked." Quickly they move among the people with malicious instruction to the crowd: Say "Barabbas!" Pilate waits; then demands an answer. At a sudden, with one accord, the crowd shouts: Barabbas! Give us Barabbas! What shall I then do with this Jesus, who

is called the Christ? demands Pilate. Crucify Him! Away with
Him! Give us Barabbas! Pilate is done. He has Jesus scourged,
robed in a purple garb, and crowned with thorns. Then he
presents Jesus the last time on the Gabbatha, saying: *Ecce
Homo!* Behold the Man! Then Pilate calls for a basin of water,
unctuously and ceremoniously has the water poured over his
hands and says: I am innocent of the blood of this just Man!
I am washing my hands clean of all this "mess."

It was then that the Jews shouted back at Pilate these
ominous words: *His blood be on us and our children!* If we
are doing anything wrong, we are ready to take the consequences!

His Blood on Us

This is the clamor of all those who reject Jesus, the Crucified. The cry came first of all from the lips of Jesus' own race,
the Jews. They, as a nation, refused to accept Jesus of Nazareth as the Messiah of God. "He came unto His own, and His
own received Him not" (John 1:11). Significantly Paul says
in Acts 28:27, 28: "For the heart of this people is waxed
gross, and their ears are dull of hearing, and their eyes have
they closed; lest they should see with their eyes, and hear with
their ears, and understand with their heart, and should be
converted and I should heal them. Be it known therefore unto
you, that the salvation of God is sent unto the Gentiles, and
that they will hear it."

In A.D. 70 Titus, Roman general, came upon Jerusalem,
besieged the city, captured it, and destroyed it and completely
demolished the Temple. With this the chosen people of the
Old Testament age and dispensation were rejected and ever
since have been known as the wandering Jews, going from
country to country, yet remaining a distinct people. By the
rejection of Jesus they have brought upon themselves as a
nation the judgment of God.

However, "His blood on us" is the cry of *all* who reject
Jesus as the Savior of the world. Jesus hung on Calvary's cross

to redeem all mankind and is pleading with all to come to Him and find forgiveness and peace. All nations, all people, all families, each one of us, one by one, are asked to come and stand beneath that cross and find healing and salvation for our sin-stained souls. But many refuse. They will not have Him, who bled and died to ransom us from the eternal separation from God. Entire nations have turned from this Jesus and closed their hearts to Him. All Asia Minor, where flourished the seven churches of Revelation, Ephesus, Smyrna, Pergamus, Thyatira, Sardis, Philadelphia, and Laodicea, are to-day in the darkness without the hope of the Gospel. It has often been said that few families remain beyond the fourth generation with the Christian church. Rejecting Him who alone can save, His blood comes to them to their damnation.

Does God not want them? Has God turned against them? No, Never! But these have turned from Him, who so loved them that He gave His only Son. Only too many say with the multitude: We need no Savior! We can take care of ourselves. We have always lived decent lives. If we are wrong, we will take the consequence! Against such stands the testimony of His blood, shed on Calvary—for only the blood of Jesus Christ, His Son, cleanseth us from all sin.

The Believer's Plea: His Blood on Us

However, "His blood on us" is the reverent and glorious plea of each and every believer of the cross. We come to God's courts, fully aware of our sins and shortcomings and failures, but we do not despair. We plead His blood. We accept that He shed His blood for us.

> Jesus, Thy blood and righteousness
> My beauty are, my glorious dress.
> Nothing in my hand I bring,
> Simply to Thy cross I cling.

His blood saves. On Calvary's tree Jesus substituted for us. He hung there, where I should have been nailed. He was forsaken that I need not be forsaken in eternity. As I am brought into the courts of God, convicted of sin, I as a believer can plead: Jesus took the blame and the guilt and the curse of *my* sin upon Himself and shed His blood as a penalty of *my* transgressions. Jesus has made good for me, paid what I could not pay, suffered the damnation of hell that I might not be separated from God forever. Jesus cleared me from all guilt and restored me to grace and favor with God in time and in eternity. All my efforts to clear myself fail; all my worrying does not pay the debt; all my tears cannot cleanse my soul. *Jesus must. Jesus did!* The blood of Jesus Christ, His Son, cleanseth me from all sin. So says Scripture. As I stand beneath this cross, His blood is on me, and for this reason only is there no condemnation for them who are in Christ Jesus. That is the faith that saves.

This is the glory of the cross; that is the glad news of Good Friday: Jesus' blood cleanses us from all sin. This salvation by His blood is offered to *all* sinners. None need go into eternity unsaved.

To-day, each day of our life, you and I are face to face with this Jesus, who was crucified on Calvary. Pilate's question is also yours and mine: What, then, shall I do with Jesus, who is called the Christ? We shall face no greater question in our life. The answer we give holds our eternal destiny. We *must do* something with Jesus. We *are* doing something with him at this very moment. We are either taking Him or Barabbas, right or wrong, falsehood or truth, darkness or light, joy or sorrow, death or life.

> When from the dust of earth I rise
> To claim my mansions in the skies;
> This then shall be my only plea:
> Jesus has bled and died for me.

With this plea and this faith in our hearts, that His blood is on us to cleanse us from all sin, we can be sure that heaven is our eternal home.

14

THE REDEEMER OF THE CROSS

> *"And the Lord laid on Him the iniquity of us all."*—Isaiah 53:6.

At Calvary we are made more than ever aware of the sinfulness of our sins. We have transgressed often and have done many things which are contrary to the will of God, and that every day of our life. We have been defeated in our battle against the evil forces of darkness which daily beset and bedraggle us. Our own bedeviled heart has nursed some pet sin and our thoughts were not thought after God.

At Calvary we are convicted by our own worthlessness as we see Jesus die on the cross. We realize that our own sins have contributed as much as those of others to the sufferings of Christ on that tree of torture. Perchance we feel more than ever that we have lived so futile and so useless that it might have been just as well had we not been born. Life seems so empty, so meaningless, so "messed up," as we commonly say. We have accomplished so little that is worthwhile, and we apparently are not needed; we are only taking up room in this world which could be put to better use by others.

Many say today: Why carry on, battling to live and making ends meet? Why resist temptations and sins when it is such an effort to conquer! What difference does it make as to what *we* do when millions crowd each other, waiting for jobs, waiting for some one to die—to make room for another. What is man anyway in this huge universe!

One of the most imposing cathedrals of the world is the Church of St. John the Divine in New York. In it have been placed nineteen statues of outstanding men of the nineteen centuries of the Christian era. The twentieth niche still remains vacant. At present no one can tell who will be placed there from among the millions and millions trudging through life in this age and time. *One*—out of the countless number—and very likely it will not be *you*. However, the Calvary message tells you and me that we are precious in God's sight, that God calls us by name and has given His only Son into the world, and laid on Him your sin and mine, that we might be His own. No one is unimportant to God. He does not want any to perish. Each one of us can look up, standing beneath the cross and say: He died *for me*. Jesus is the *world's* Redeemer, but He is also *my* Savior, for the Lord laid on Him the iniquity *of us all*.

All Sin Laid Upon One

We want to ponder, then, as we stand on Calvary, upon the stupendous fact that the sin of the whole world was laid on Jesus. That is why John the Baptist said: "Behold the Lamb of God, which taketh away the sin of the world!" (John 1:29). The people of John's day fully appreciated the significance of this statement. John was referring to the sacrificial lamb which was offered upon the Temple altar at Jerusalem to make atonement for Israel's sin.

Once a year all Israel observed the day of Atonement, known in modern time as Yom Kippur (cf. Leviticus 16:29–34). On this Atonement Day the high priest, garbed in a white linen garment, approached the Altar of Sacrifice which stood in front of the Temple, visible from all parts of the surrounding courts. On his chest hung the breastplate adorned with twelve precious stones. On each of the stones was inscribed the name of one of the tribes of Israel. As the high priest ascended to the altar, a Levite brought a lamb, one year old, and placed it upon the altar. For fourteen days this lamb had been examined to make sure that the animal was without blemish or scar. Physically it must be perfect. Then the high priest would lay his hand upon the animal, symbolizing that Israel's sins were laid upon this "innocent" lamb. Next the high priest would reach for a knife and proceed to cut the lamb's throat from ear to ear. Thus its blood was shed, and it died for the sins of the people. Some of this blood was caught up in a vessel with which the high priest would enter into the temple. First he passed through the Holies of the Temple, where stood the altar of incense, the table of shewbread, and the candlestick. Parting the veil which separated the Holies from the Most Holies, he would enter this Sacred Room, into which he was permitted to go only this one time each year. In the Most Holies stood the Ark of Covenant, which contained besides the pot of manna and the rod of Aaron the two stones on which Moses had written the Ten Commandments by the direction of God. On this ark was a cover, called the Mercy Seat, on which stood two angels, facing each other. The blood which the high priest brought into the Most Holies was now sprinkled over the Mercy Seat. We ask why?

This was to announce to the people that blood had been shed for the sins which Israel had committed against these Commandments of the Lord. Something had died for Israel. All this was a type of the Messiah who had been promised already in the Garden of Eden and who was to give His life as a ransom for sin, which sin God had laid on Him. As Jesus appears at the beginning of His ministry at Bethabara John announces to Israel and to us that this Jesus of Nazareth is the *Messiah-Lamb* who is to die for the sin of the world.

Every Sin is Ugly and Damning

All this is to tell you and me, as we stand at the cross, that sin is the most damaging and soul-destroying thing which comes into our lives. All that is evil and wicked and damning in our conduct and in our world is caused by sin. Sin is the ugliest thing in God's creation world. The heartaches which darken our days, the cruelties which torture the souls of men, the brutalities of man's inhumanity to man, the crimes of a godless society in form of murder, adultery, theft, arson, and what not, are due to sin. All our sins are a violation against the Ten Commandments of our Jehovah-Lord. As we are aware of the destructiveness of sin, we blush at our own and are ashamed of the inhuman acts of our fellowmen. We need not look far to find sin, even in ourselves. If we say we have never sinned, we are deceiving no one but ourselves. Scratch beneath the surface of our own lives and we see sin in every form and device: gloating over the downfall of others, planning spiteful revenge, discrediting others with slurring and cutting remarks, We know best—for our conscience points the finger at us—how and when we have sinned. Therefore Jesus says: "Out of the heart proceed evil thoughts" and then catalogs the ugly things we say and do.

However, we shall never understand nor fathom the damnableness of sin until we come to the cross and see Jesus dying for our transgressions. In that darkness of Calvary He pays the penalty for sin and sheds His innocent blood for our redemption. At the cross we see that every sin, even the most insignificant, judged by the standard of man, puts a dark line into God's face and causes untold agony to the body and soul of Jesus. Only at Calvary's cross we realize how awful is our transgression against the law of Sinai. We must confess with David: "Against Thee, Thee only, have I sinned, and done this evil in Thy sight" (Psalm 51:4).

All Sin on Jesus

All this sin was laid on Jesus. He took it away that God should see sin no more and blot it out of His remembrance. Sin and transgression cannot go unchallenged. Sin must be punished if the holiness of God is to stand. The Bible teaches this. Sin drove Adam and Eve out of Paradise. Sin put a mark on Cain's forehead. Sin brought trouble into Abraham's household. Sin sent Absalom to an ignoble death under a heap of stones. Sin made the rich young ruler walk away sorrowful. Sin made Ananias and Sapphira tell the untruth about the value of their property. Sin made Gehazi steal and lie about his theft. Sin made Demas love this present world more than Paul's Gospel. All these sins were punished. Nature teaches the same truth. Drink to excess, eat as a glutton, break the laws of health, and you learn to your sorrow that the way of the transgressor is hard.

Even our own conscience rises as witness against us and tells us that our sins will bring upon us the judgments of God and man. So the guilty hide out and do their evil deeds in the dark. The robber flees and the thief is afraid of his own shadow. Sin condemns man in time and in eternity.

Punishment and Forgiveness, Opposites

Punishment, therefore, is the very opposite of mercy, pardon, forgiveness. Justice and mercy are not bedfellows. If sin is punished in me, then sin is not forgiven. If my sin is forgiven me, then I am not punished. How can these two facts and truths be reconciled? The answer is found in our text: "The Lord laid on Him [the Lamb of God], the iniquity of us all."

If I am to go unpunished for my sins, I need a Savior who will take the blame upon Himself and pay the penalty of my transgression. I cannot pay the death penalty and live. And Scripture definitely says: "The soul that sinneth it shall die."

The only solution, then, to my sin problem is found on Calvary. There the Lord laid on Him, His sinless Son, my sin. Therefore Jesus substituted for me. His suffering was more than an example of patient endurance of pain. Jesus' agony is more than a rising above suffering and conquering pain by gritting His teeth. His suffering was a payment for sins He never committed and yet took upon Himself. It was *my* sin which caused Him to be forsaken, to thirst, to suffer excruciating pain. He did not want us to go through these agonies, for we would have perished in them. And the glory of this truth and Gospel is this, that Isaiah tells us in his message from God, that the Lord laid on Him the iniquity of us *all*. This *"all"* leaves no one out. It closes the door on none living in this present world. No exceptions are listed. This I must believe, if I am to have peace of mind. God's love and Christ's sacrifice must include me. *All* sinners, great and small; all criminals and all saints; thieves and priests, Pharisees and publicans, for one and all, Jesus died on the cross of Calvary and shed His blood as the Lamb of God and the Redeemer of the world.

The Most Hopeful Message of Time

The Gospel of Calvary is the most hopeful message ever proclaimed to man. Many victors have returned to their people to be welcomed home in triumphal joy. But what spelled victory to one nation meant defeat and submission and bondage to those over whom the victory was won. However, the message of the cross is a glad news which tells every human being that his Victor has won. Not one single soul is left out. That Altar of Calvary is for everybody. Everybody can come. Above all, important to us is this fact, that *we* can come. "The Lord laid on Him the iniquity of us *all.*" "And with His stripes *we* are healed." Here is the *world's* Redeemer. Therefore John the Baptist, seeing Jesus for the first time, says to the multitude at Bethabara: "Behold the Lamb of God, which taketh away the sin of the *world.*"

But Behold!

But you and I must behold. We must look to Him who was wounded and died for us. Just as the Israelites in the wilderness had to look up to the brazen serpent to escape death (Numbers 21:9), even so we *must* look up to Christ Crucified to be healed from sin. There is no other way of escape; only through this Jesus are we washed and cleansed. If we are not restored to grace at the cross, refuse to come there and look up to the dying Redeemer, then death and damnation is our lot throughout all eternity. Now is the

day of salvation. Death closes the door to heaven if we refuse
to behold *now* this Savior who was wounded for our transgressions.

Therefore, John the Baptist says: "Behold!" Look and live.
Then we can go through this world with peace in our heart
and abide in eternity with this crucified yet living Christ,
who is King forever and ever. Look, for you cannot make
me believe that you have never sinned. Even your own conscience will not accept such a claim. The voice within rises
as witness to speak against you and places on you the blame
of your sinful acts. However, as you are sprinkled with the
blood of the Lamb of God there *is* cleansing and healing
from all sin. At the cross there are no unforgiven sins, nor
unforgivable sins.

On Calvary God in Christ stands at the door of your heart
and pleads: "Come now, and let us reason together, saith the
Lord: though your sins be as scarlet, they shall be as white
as snow; though they be red like crimson, they shall be as
wool" (Isaiah 1:18). "He will abundantly pardon" (Isaiah
55:7). Therefore, *my name* and *yours* are written in the Book
of Life and *we* are heirs of all that is eternal.

> Drawn to the cross, which Thou hast blessed
> With healing gifts for souls distressed,
> To find in Thee my life, my rest
> Christ Crucified, I come.
>
> Wash me and take away each stain;
> Let nothing of my sin remain;
> For cleansing, though it be through pain,
> Christ Crucified, I come!

15

THE EMPTY TOMB OF THE CROSS

> *"And very early in the morning, the first day*
> *of the week, they came unto the sepulchre*
> *at the rising of the sun. And they said among*
> *themselves, Who shall roll us away the*
> *stone from the door of the sepulchre? And*
> *when they looked, they saw that the stone*
> *was rolled away; for it was very great."*
> —Mark 16:2-4.

The resurrection of Jesus is the most challenging fact in history. It is a miracle of such tremendous moment that it makes every other phenomenon fade into insignificance. Man has accomplished astounding successes. Nothing seems to surprise us as we hear of new discoveries and read of more recent inventions. We take all for granted. We would not be surprised to hear that some one reached the moon. We have lived in an age of miracles: The telephone, the radio, the television, atomic energy, automation. *But no one has ever raised himself from the dead.* None but Jesus.

The resurrection makes the most daring demand on our faith. If we accept that Jesus is risen from the dead, then we cannot consistently reject any of the revelations of the Bible, for Jesus put the stamp of genuineness on all that is in the Bible, saying: "The Scripture cannot be broken" (John 10:35).

Every effort certainly was made to remove every possibility of deception. The leaders of Jerusalem made sure that no hoax be played on them by the disciples or sympathetic friends of Jesus. We truly are thankful for all these precautions. Those who had succeeded in having Jesus crucified and put to death also made sure that this Jesus who was put into the tomb of Joseph of Arimathea would remain there. They had the sepulchre sealed by the state and guarded by soldiers of the government. Mark, who gives us the earliest written account of the life and death and resurrection of Jesus, records: And the women coming early in the morning to the sepulchre say to one another: Who shall roll away the large stone from the sepulchre? As they look they notice that the stone is rolled aside. The seal is broken, the soldiers gone, and as they look into the tomb, it is empty. Mark stresses three facts: The stone was heavy, it was sealed; it was guarded. Yet on that first day of the week, when the women come at sunrise to the place where Jesus had been laid to rest, *the stone is rolled away.*

The Heavy Stone is Moved

Much is made over the fact that the heavy stone was moved. The women admit that it was too heavy for them to roll aside from the door. It would therefore be folly to argue that these women tampered with this huge stone and opened the tomb. The women hardly would dare to try to roll the stone away because it had been sealed by the government. This had been done at the request of the Jerusalem leaders. They came to Pilate, saying: "Sir, we remember that that deceiver said, while He was yet alive, After three days I will rise again. Command therefore that the sepulchre be made sure until the third day, lest His disciples come by night, and steal Him away, and say unto the people, He is risen from the dead: so the last error shall be worse than the first. Pilate said unto them, Ye have a watch [You have a guard of soldiers, RSV]: go your way, make it as sure as ye can" (Matthew 27:63—65) . And that is what the leaders did.

This stone, then, was sealed by the authority of the state. That removed any possibility of the women having tampered with the seal and stone; or the disciples, who at that time "were scared to death," as we commonly say.

The Guarded Stone

The stone was guarded. The soldiers who were assigned to this duty were under the strict discipline of the Roman army. They would allow no one to come near, if they had such orders. They walked to and fro in front of the tomb day and night, for twenty-four hours. Yet the stone was moved that early morning from the opening in the sepulchre. The soldiers report so to the officials under whose authority they were assigned to this duty. They tell of the earthquake and the moving of the stone and that the tomb was empty when they looked in.

The women likewise report the removal of the stone to the disciples, and Mary Magdalene is sure that the body had been stolen by unfriendly hands. John and Peter, therefore, hurry to the place to see what really had happened.

The Empty Tomb

As Peter and John entered the sepulchre they found the linens which had been wrapped about the body of Jesus carefully laid and the napkin which had been placed over the face of Jesus was folded and laid aside by itself. This indicated that there had been no vandalism nor any hasty activity by evil-minded persons. But the fact stands that the stone was rolled away from the opening and that the tomb was empty. The soldiers say so; Peter and John say so; Mary Magdalene and the other women say so.

What caused the stone to be moved? Nothing less than the hand of God. The seal was broken by God, and *not* by man. And *why* was this stone rolled from the door? To show that the tomb was really empty. The body of the Lord, which was laid there on Friday evening, was no longer there. The Lord Jesus had risen as He said He would. And this resurrection took place within three days and Jesus was seen by those who could identify Him as One with whom they had associated for years. They knew Him so well that they were positive that this Jesus whom they saw *after* the resurrection was the same Jesus who was crucified and died on Calvary. So the stone was moved to proclaim to all mankind the crowning miracle of Jesus. To this day we can rejoice and sing: *Christ is risen! Hallelujah!*

The Risen Christ is Lord God

This resurrection of Jesus clinches for all time to come His claim that He is the Son of God, God of very God. This was to be the standard miracle and proof of the divine origin of Jesus, called by Himself, the sign of the prophet Jonah. If He rose, then He must be the Messiah-God, come into the world, made flesh, to free humanity from the dominion and power of Satan and sin. This claim, proven by indisputable evidences, compels us to fall to our knees and say with Thomas: "My Lord and my God!" We cannot do otherwise, if we are honest with ourselves. This resurrection proves conclusively that Jesus *is* the living and abiding Lord, who is the Head of His Church and the King of time and eternity.

Truth Triumphs

The resurrection clinches the claim that truth triumphs. Jesus had been maligned by the Sanhedrin and many others, even by some of His kinfolk. They said, He has the devil; others, He is beside Himself. He has hallucinations of bigness and self-importance. But the resurrection proves that He is God, and His Word is Truth.

This Gospel is discredited by many to this day. They claim that it is an opiate which is to soothe us into submission that the church might control our lives. This is branded as a lie by the resurrection of Jesus. He gives a genuine hope to mankind, as He announces: Because I live, ye shall live also. The truth is always winning out. Jesus' influence keeps the world in balance to this very day. Each year the dreary and disturbed people put aside their gloom and rejoicingly sing: Christ is risen! Hallelujah!

The Great Rock

The rock that moved on that first Easter morn gives us the continued assurance that we have a *Rock of Ages* upon whom we are building all our hopes in life, in death, in eternity. Jesus' resurrection is the key which opens every prison house of sin and sets us free to live in the grace of God daily. All trouble we have in this world, be it in nation, communities, or families, is due to sin. The guilt complex which causes thousands and ten thousands of restless nights and the fear of judgment to come is due to sin. Sin is real and sin is ugly and sin is damning. The tragic fact about sin is this, that all the waters of the earth cannot wash out the "damned spots" of sin.

> Not the labors of my hands
> Can fulfil Thy law's demands.

Jesus came to rescue man from the power of sin by taking for us the "beating" as He was wounded for our transgression on the cross. That is the significance of Calvary. He died for us. However, and mark this well, the crucifixion would be just another tragic story of "man's inhumanity to man" if Jesus had remained in the grave. *But He rose.* This is God's proclamation to man that the sin-debt is wiped out and we are released from the bondage of hell. Only our obstinacy keeps us in the dungeon to perish in unbelief.

Our New Life in Christ

The resurrection of Jesus is the key which opens up to us a new life in time and hereafter. As believers in the risen Lord we are transformed into new beings. Old things have passed away. We rise to a newness of life with Christ in our hearts. We have a new love, new interests, a new freedom, a new joy. In this world we are living already in the spiritual resurrection, dead to trespasses and sin. This makes us incorruptible. This holds out for us another resurrection, when this sin-ridden and dying body shall rise to be like His glorious

body. Ours is a personal resurrection. This dust-body shall
live beyond the allotted time of this world.

Therefore, we can face death without fear. Our death has
been made into a sleep by Jesus, and certainly we are not
afraid to go to sleep! Rather we covet sleep after a day's activity. We believers fall asleep in death to be awakened in a
glory that is endless. What comfort to those whose household
has been visited by the angel of death! Your loved ones are
in glory. There we shall meet again. That is the promise of
the risen Lord. The resurrection of Jesus gives us an emphatic
yes to the age-old question: If a man die, shall he live again?
This is not wishful thinking, but a glorious truth which
puts hope into our hearts as we are in sorrow and in tears.

There is a Church Triumphant

The resurrection of Jesus is the key which opens the door
to the church triumphant. At present the church is harrassed
by enemies from without and within. The indifference of
its adherents is one of the great menaces to the church. Such
lukewarm Christianity does the church no good. Still more:
the church is often disturbed by persecution and then by
ridicule. Often we ask: Will the church survive? The risen
Lord makes certain that He who is the living Head and the
almighty God will never allow the forces of evil to crush
His Gospel. His church will go on from victory to victory
until the church becomes the triumphant church of eternity.

Real Gospel

The resurrection of Jesus, then, gives us a genuine Gospel,
a glad news which never lets us down. And what is its basic
message? This Gospel proclaims to us that we are reconciled
to God and have a peace that passes human understanding;
we have a hope which lets us look always upward with confidence and even at the portals of death and eternity tells us
that there is no condemnation for them who are in Christ
Jesus. Above all, this risen Lord promises to meet us on the

other shore to welcome us home as pilgrims of the way to live with Him forever.

This good news the world of today needs desperately if it is to have any hope. Many ideologies pose as Gospel to human society, making endless promises of a perfect world in this present time, in which every one will have his fill of good things and that without much effort. However, in the end these ideologies let us down as we realize that there is no pot of gold at the end of the rainbow. Even our vaunted democracies have their putrid sores which smell to high heaven.

However, this resurrection Gospel promises us something that all the diamonds of Golconda cannot buy and all the powers of the world cannot give. Every known ideology holds out something for this world—and we know that all that is earthly is shaken out of our dying hands all too soon. We cannot deny that most people are eking out a bare existence on a minimum of earthly possessions. They have little of that which is called success and affluence. Jesus' resurrection promises, "Because I live, ye shall live also," and "In Thy presence is fulness of joy." What more can we ask?

Here then is a glad message which brings peace to the heart, cleansing to the soul, hope in the hour of death, and a salvation which never ends.

Let us, then, go home and sing all this week the joyous melody: "Christ is risen! Hallelujah!"

16

THE EASTER TRIUMPH OF THE CROSS

"And if Christ be not raised, your faith is vain, ye are yet in your sins. Then they also which are fallen asleep in Christ, are perished. If in this life only we have hope in Christ, we are of all men most miserable. But now is Christ risen from the dead, and become the firstfruits of them that slept. For since by man came death, by man came also the resurrection of the dead. For as in Adam all die, even so in Christ shall all be made alive."
—1 Corinthians 15:17-22.

Easter is the brightest spot on the horizon of our life. No greater morning has dawned upon the world and history than that Easter when the tomb of Joseph of Arimathea was empty and Jesus was seen alive at five different times that first day of the week. Easter tells us of a greater miracle than that of spring with its new-born leaf and flower, sunshine and warmth. Easter answers the age-old question, which Job asked in the childhood of the world: "If a man die, shall he live again?" (Job 14:14) . The risen Lord of Easter morn replies with the positive assurance: "Because I live, ye shall live also." The Easter message is death-defying, giving hope beyond the grave and the portals of eternity. Easter gives us an expectancy that no sorrow can dim and no world upheaval can destroy.

Easter enabled martyrs of the first century to stand at Caesar's stall in the Roman arena and exclaim as they faced the hungry lions: "Hail, Caesar! We who are about to die salute

thee!" Death had lost its sting, fear and uncertainty fled from
the Christian hearts, all because they knew and believed that
Jesus rose the third day from the dead. Easter proclaims the
mightiest act of God's omnipotence, greater than that of the
creation of the world.

With triumphant exaltation Paul exclaims: "But now *is*
Christ risen from the dead. Thanks be to God who giveth us
the victory through our Lord Jesus Christ."

Who Won?

Who won the victory? Here is Paul's answer: "But now is
Christ risen from the dead." This is the answer—positive,
clear, certain, as plain as day.

Jesus, who won the victory, had said during His public
ministry that He would. He was His own *prophet* who foretold this all important and most significant event as a proof
of His Messiahship. At one time certain scribes and Pharisees
came to Jesus, demanding of Him a sign or miracle which
would prove conclusively that He is the Son of God and the
Messiah of promise. At that occasion Jesus made this prophetic statement: "There shall no sign be given to it [this
generation] but the sign of the prophet Jonas. For as Jonas
was three days and three nights in the whale's belly, so shall
the Son of man be three days and three nights in the heart
of the earth" (Matthew 12:39, 40). On another occasion,
when Jesus drove the money changers off the temple site, the
Jews at Jerusalem said to Him: "What sign showest Thou
unto us?" (John 2:18). To that Passover crowd Jesus replied:
"Destroy this temple, and in three days I will raise it up"
(John 2:19). Jesus knew from the beginning that He would
die and rise again. On Easter morn, then, with the rising of
the sun, Jesus came forth from Joseph's tomb, proclaiming
His victory over death and thereby declaring that He was
more than a prophet—that He was the Son of God. Death
could not hold its Lord. He is the Resurrection and the Life.

Christ who triumphed on Easter morn was likewise the

great *High priest* who on the altar of Calvary sacrificed Himself as the Lamb of God. God had laid on Him the iniquity of us all, and Jesus went down into death and hell to pay the penalty for sin and free us from the curse of the Sinai Law. To His disciples Jesus said as they went with Him to that final Passover: "Behold, we go up to Jerusalem, and all things that are written by the prophets concerning the Son of man shall be accomplished. For He shall be delivered unto the Gentiles, and shall be mocked, and spitefully entreated, and spitted on: And they shall scourge Him, and put Him to death; and the third day He shall rise again" (Luke 18:31-33). Jesus gave His life on Calvary's cross and shed His blood to make atonement for sin. That was the specific purpose of this crucifixion. His resurrection, therefore, is God's proclamation that His Son has accomplished what He set out to do. He won the victory and triumphed over the power of darkness on Easter morning and set all mankind free. Man is redeemed and sin is forgiven and life eternal is ours who believe and accept these terms of salvation. Jesus has crushed Satan's head.

Christ who won the Easter victory and triumphed over Satan, sin, and death is now *King* of kings and of eternity. Satan is defeated and is bound already in this New Testament age, for the gates of hell cannot destroy even the Church Militant of which the risen Jesus is the Head, the Bishop, and the Ruler. Satan cannot deceive or destroy Christ's elect. And when time ends and eternity begins His faithful shall live and reign with Christ in an everlasting glory of eternity.

Therefore the Easter triumph tells you and me that we have a Savior who loves and preserves us in His grace until journey's end. He has set us free from the condemning judgment of the Law and placed us into His kingdom of grace, where the sunshine of His love and the healing of His righteousness preserves us in that faith which saves. We believers stand in His grace, where daily we are washed, cleansed, healed, and clothed in His holiness. Sin cannot defeat us, Satan cannot claim us, death has no stranglehold on us to consign us forever to the grave. When the King of glory returns with His holy angels on that last day, then my dust-body shall rise to be made like His glorious body. Then sin, pain, sorrow, and death cannot touch me again. I shall live in His presence where there is a fullness of joy which shall never be dimmed or marred. Jesus' Easter triumph means glory for me.

> When from the dust of death I rise
> To claim my mansions in the skies,
> E'en then this shall be all my plea:
> Jesus hath lived and died for me.

The Easter Triumph Important

This Easter triumph of Jesus, then, is of the greatest significance for you and me. The clinching grip of death is broken. "But now is Christ risen from the dead, and become the first fruits of them that slept." Just what does Paul want to stress by calling Jesus *"the first fruits?"*

The Old Testament Ceremonial Law required that Israel would pluck the fruits which first ripened on the tree and the grain which yellowed first in the field and bring these as a thankoffering to God. These first fruits were a recognition of God's goodness toward the people. However, more was to be emphasized. These first ripening fruits and grain were God's assurance that the remainder of the harvest would ripen in due time and provide for the people's need. In like manner is the resurrection of Jesus, as the first, to be a guarantee to us Christians that we too shall rise from the dead with a glorious body like unto that of the risen Lord.

Death Temporary

The believer's death is a temporary sleep from which this body, returning to dust, shall be awakened to be clothed in a perfection that sin cannot touch. This takes the fear out of death and dying. With Simeon we can say: "Lord, now

lettest Thou Thy servant depart in peace" (Luke 2:29).
With David we can look death in the face and say: "Yea,
though I walk through the valley of the shadow of death,
I will fear no evil, for Thou art with me" (Psalm 23:4).
Our imperfect and sin-harrassed body shall rest from the toiling and trials of life until the resurrection morning of eternity.

Still more. The resurrection of Jesus gives us the assurance
of peace with God and with this peace a good conscience.
Paul says that if Christ be raised, then, we are no more in
sin (cf. verse 17). We are living in grace as believers, justified before God through the blood of the risen Christ. Sin is
taken off our shoulders. Christ has paid in full. Therefore
we are acquitted. This makes the outlook of our daily life
brighter. We can lift our eyes upward in faith and look forward with courage. No matter what we might have to face
as pilgrims of the Way in this world and life, we cannot
perish. That is the promise. Daily we are washed and healed
from sin and upheld by His everlasting hands.

Therefore, the resurrection of Jesus guarantees to us a
home with God and gives us the certainty and the confidence
which will not let us down. Even when we stand at the
portals of death and eternity we still can hope. This frail,
sickly, aging, dying, body racked in pain, shall live and be
like the body of our risen Lord. "For since by man came
death, by Man [Christ] came also the resurrection of the dead.
For as in Adam all die, even so in Christ shall all be made
alive."

Eternity Permanent

Our earthly life is short, checkered by endless uncertainties and limitations. In the resurrection our life shall be stabilized and permanently settled in an eternity of heaven from
which the believer, washed white in the blood of the Lamb,
shall never be asked to move. Death then is the door to the
homeland.

Frances R. Havergal, who has written many Christian

hymns, which have found their way into our hymnals, was handicapped for many years with poor health. However, she has written a number of beautiful hymns expressing her faith and hope, because the risen Lord dwelt in her heart. With confidence and courage she sang in her physical imprisonment:

> I am trusting Thee, Lord Jesus,
> Trusting only Thee;
> Trusting Thee for full salvation
> Great and free.

Her life was dedicated to Christ whose abiding presence filled her heart with peace and contentment. Therefore she could sing:

> Take my life, and let it be
> Consecrated Lord, to Thee:
> Take my love, my Lord, I pour
> At Thy feet its treasure store;
> Take myself, and I will be,
> Ever, only, all for Thee.

When the morning of eternity comes, Jesus, the risen Lord, stands on the other shore to welcome us home. And we need not be afraid to face Him, for there is no condemnation for them who are in Christ Jesus (cf. Romans 8:1).

What difference this faith in the risen Lord makes in us! We begin a new, transformed life *now*. We are new creatures, risen to a newness of life with a new purpose, zeal, and goal. Note what transformation took place in the Twelve! They had hidden behind bolted doors. They were afraid to be seen on the streets of Jerusalem after dark. Then they saw the risen Lord. He commissioned them to go everywhere to tell the Gospel of the cross and resurrection. Filled with a zeal and a conviction that no one could take from them, they went forth to tell throughout the Roman Empire the resurrection story which has turned the world upside down. They possessed a joy, a hope, a security, a faith unshaken.

They were sure. Peter expresses this faith in his first Epistle: "Blessed be God and Father of our Lord Jesus Christ, which according to His abundant mercy hath begotten us again unto a lively [living or permanent] hope by the resurrection of Jesus Christ from the dead to an inheritance incorruptible, and undefiled, and that fadeth not away, reserved in heaven for you, who are kept by the power of God through faith unto salvation ready to be revealed in the last time."

Death Does Not Stop Christians

Death can stop many things and many persons. Death stopped Alexander, Napoleon, Hitler, Stalin, and thousands of others. But death does not stop the Christian. He goes through the valley up to the great white throne to sing the Easter Hallelujahs of heaven.

That is the reason why Easter is the great day of Triumph. Science does not know what lies beyond the grave and in eternity. Philosophy has no answer to Job's question: "If a man die, shall he live again?" The longing of the heart and yearnings of the soul ask with Hamlet in Shakespeare's tragedy:

> To be or not to be,—that is the question.
> To die,—to sleep,—perchance to dream,—
> Ah, there's the rub!

Jesus has the answer. The risen Lord comes to us and promises: "Because I live, ye shall live also." Since Jesus is risen, Paul argues, that never again can we Christians be really miserable in this life. If Christ is *not* risen, then, of course, we have no hope. But Christ *is* risen. Therefore, we need not and cannot despair. If Christ is not risen, then it is true, says Paul, that all perish who die. This is not a pleasant thought. That would make life a most tragic experience for most of us. But Christ *is* risen, says the Easter Message. If so, then we cannot perish, who are Christ's own.

So the Easter triumph is the brightest spot on the horizon of life. We know that Jesus stands on the other shore of eternity as the risen Lord with healing in His pierced hands, holding out a hope that enables us to say with an unshaken conviction: I believe in the resurrection of the body and life everlasting. Heaven is my home. Although the message of the cross still stands Jesus is no longer nailed to the cross in death, but lives in a glory that is without end.